Your Life Together

Your Life Together

© 2010 Christian Book Council

All Rights Reserved.

Address:

KRE Book Group

PO Box 121135

Nashville, TN 37212-1135

TABLE OF CONTENTS

DEDICATION 5

WHO SHOULD GO ON THE JOURNEY? 7

THE MEANING OF MARRIAGE 23

PLANNING IN ADVANCE 35

THE TWO TRAVELERS 43

THE FIRST TWO YEARS 59

THE LOVE RELATIONSHIP 81

ADDING TO THE PARTY 95

DIFFICULTIES ON THE WAY 107

DANGEROUS CROSSROADS 129

THE MIDDLE YEARS 139

CAN RELIGION HELP? 157

JOURNEY'S END 165

DEDICATION

This book is dedicated to all of those entering the school for living known as marriage.

Your Life Together

WHO SHOULD GO ON THE JOURNEY?

Marriage is an adventure.

It is not a straightforward, direct journey from one point to another. It is not so much an institution as a way of living. Thus in marriage, as in life, there is no standing still; life moves forward all the time—so does marriage.

This article is a guide to the journey of marriage, but it is not a conducted tour. As marriage is essentially a part of living, nobody can solve for you all the problems you will meet on the way. The one who humbly tries to help you can only indicate the right direction, point out some of the dangers, make practical suggestions—then leave you to it.

Learning Marriage

To a great extent you have to learn marriage as you go along. It is very important to recognize this at the start. If we could embark upon marriage fully aware of all its demands, the whole subject of marriage guidance would be much simpler than it is. But then marriage would cease to be an adventure. We would know from the outset precisely what to expect. We should need only to comply with rules drawn up in advance to be certain of getting along satisfactorily.

No people who marry, whether for love or otherwise, begin by knowing all they need to know about life or marriage. This is because there is so much to be learned in marriage which cannot possibly be learned outside it. True, we can learn some things by study or by closely observing other marriages. But in a practical sense what matters most to us can be learned in only one way—in the school of our own day-to-day marriage experience.

Every marriage involves two persons; and no two human beings are absolutely identical; so no two marriages are alike. Moreover, in every marriage there is a partnership of two persons of opposite sex; and the sexes are not alike. In addition to the obvious physical differences there are emotional and mental differences which, in the main, are not so obvious. These reveal themselves in attitudes and actions, and are of the utmost importance. It is therefore hardly surprising that the degree of adaptability and re-adaptability of each partner to the other varies in different marriages.

The goal is a happy union lasting through life. Its attainment depends mainly upon the degree of adjustment achieved by each of the partners. That is why marriage is really the art of human relationship at its best. It means learning by experience how to adapt yourself to your husband or wife so that there is real co-operation on every plane—physical, mental, emotional, and spiritual. To be a "good mixer" or a good cooperator in general is not enough, although the qualities which make for such social graces may materially aid your marriage. You must acquire the art of happy adjustment not only to people in general, but *to your husband or wife.*

This may seem obvious; but some people find it hard to believe that marriage is really a school in which we learn the art of

> You must acquire the art of happy adjustment not only to people in general, but your husband or wife.

living together in the most intimate way. They feel that they already know everything that really matters. They see in marriage merely the opportunity to *apply* what they already know.

Now it may seem of minor importance, but really it is absolutely vital that those who embark upon marriage should fully recognize that they have a great deal to learn about themselves in relation to their partners, and about their partners in relation to themselves. It is worth while here devoting a little attention to this extremely important aspect.

"Know-Alls" Who Fail

Life's most valuable lessons are usually learned slowly. Those who find it difficult, if not impossible, to accept the idea of a lengthy process of enlightenment arising from day-to-day experience in marriage usually fall within one of the following groups:

1) The sexual type who places undue emphasis upon the physical aspect of marriage;

2) The idealist who is under the influence of the romantic illusion, which makes it impossible for him to regard marriage in a rational manner;

3) The anxiety type who, influenced by propaganda or by observation of marriages which have failed, is profoundly convinced that the scales are heavily weighted against any marriage proving really happy.

It may appear rather harsh to lump all these together in the "know-all" class. But that is really where they belong. For although the individuals who compose these groups include all types of character and temperament they have one thing in common. They all see marriage as a fixed, unchanging pattern. They all feel that they know in advance what will happen.

That they should think and feel this way may not be their own fault. "Life"—their experiences from the day they were born—have made them what they are. But as their attitude is completely at variance with what is needed to make a success of marriage we must examine its several facets in some detail.

1) The Sexual Type

Those who place undue emphasis on the physical aspect of marriage are usually (but not always) men. Woman's deepest nature differs from men. With her, in the large majority of cases,

Who Should Go On The Journey?

everything is subordinate to the mother urge which Nature has given her. This is her driving force in life. Consequently sex, in its narrower sense of physical sexual expression, does not obtrude to anything like the degree it so often reaches in a man's life.

It is hardly surprising that many tend to place strong emphasis on the sexual aspect when contemplating marriage, since they lack a sound understanding of the all-embracing nature of the marital union. For at puberty both youths and girls are physically ready for marriage. They experience the urge to unite with a member of the opposite sex. But Society in general and parents in particular, insist that this should be expressed only in marriage.

There are various sound reasons for this. The most important of them can be classified as (a) Economic; and (b) Psychological.

(a) A youth permitted to run wild and indulge in sexual intercourse whenever he felt the urge might impregnate a large number of females. But he would not, unless his was a very exceptional case, earn enough to maintain any one of them—let alone any children.

This economic reason for Society's insistence upon delay is by no means the more important. The numerous children who would be born to very young parents could not possibly be properly cared for by the only people capable by nature of caring for them most effectively—their own parents.

(b)   The psychological aspect is of primary importance because we learn the art of living in the school of life, and very young people still have much to learn. They need to know a good deal more of the world and its ways before they are fitted to have children. Few adolescent boys or girls have learned enough of human relationships to be able to discharge satisfactorily the responsibilities of parenthood, which are, when all is said and done, the heaviest responsibilities which human beings can assume. Society therefore demands that marriage be deferred until there is at least a reasonable prospect of the partners having gained a sufficient acquaintance with the everyday problems facing all adults. In other words, *physical* maturity is recognized by Church, State, and public opinion generally as being inadequate by itself. Some degree of *emotional* maturity is also essential if the partners are to stand a sound chance of building a happy marriage relationship and bringing up a happy family. Looked at in this way, Society's attitude is seen to be not unreasonable.

Who Should Go On The Journey? 15

The fact remains that young people are physically ready to mate as soon as puberty has been attained. Thus there is a conflict between their individual inner urges on the one hand and the collective attitude conditioned by Society on the other. With Nature strongly urging them to do one thing and Society equally strongly forbidding it, many become impatient to marry. They feel that marriage is a sort of license to indulge in physical sexual expression, which has hitherto been denied them. And some of them enter the marriage relationship with this narrow, limited outlook. They measure the success or otherwise of their marriage mainly, if not entirely, by the gauge of its physical achievement.

A marriage relationship based solely on physical unity must soon become boring; this has been proved by many couples who once thought otherwise. They have learned the fallacy of such a belief in the hard school of experience, often in the course of years of miserable existence. And there are still some who believe that "sex" is what matters most.

2) The Idealist

This is a form of physical attraction combined with ignorance of what marriage involves. It varies considerably in degree, from the intense infatuation of the person who is "madly in love" to the mild tinge of romantic illusion present in the emotional outlook of many people. In its extreme form the victim develops a completely distorted view of the object of affection. When a young man of this type falls in love, he sees the girl as an ideal creature, possessing only charms and virtues. She is, as others can plainly see, an ordinary human being, and, like all human beings, she is far from perfect. A girl of this type who falls in love sees her beloved only through rose-tinted spectacles, and although others may point out that he has many faults and may, indeed, be quite unsuitable as a husband, she can worship only one whose apparent gifts and virtues are far beyond anything ever encountered in real life.

The trouble is that infatuation does not last. The very intensity of the emotion usually results in its being short-lived. And once infatuation has passed, the victims become clear-eyed again and are able to see each other as ordinary human beings. It is no exaggeration to say that infatuated people are in love with dream products of their own imaginations. Some small trait or physical peculiarity may account for the original attraction, and upon that frail pedestal is erected a model of perfection which does not exist outside the infatuated person's own imagination.

Who Should Go On The Journey?

Romantic idealism is fostered by numerous novels, plays, films, poems, and popular songs which merely retell, in sophisticated language, the fairy stories which made grownup life seem so very easy and pleasant when we were very young. But a far greater influence than all of these is the power of parental guidance. Many parents tend to talk to their children in terms of a great love, as though this might be expected to come to them and cast its warmth over their lives, unmindful of the truth, or else forgetful of it, that love which lasts usually has to be carefully tended. It is infinitely better for parents to recognize and stress the plain truth, that marriage is essentially a practical matter. The more young people realize that marriage involves the acceptance of duties and responsibilities, and above all that it involves an understanding and application of the rules of good human relationships, the fewer romantic idealists there will be to marry and come to grief.

This brings us to the very heart of the matter. Husbands and wives, whatever faults or merits they possess, do not act like goblins but as flesh-and-blood men and women. They do not live ideal lives, but have their imperfections. Those who marry with these facts well in mind and fully appreciated stand a fair chance of success. They know that they have a task to perform, and that their ultimate success or failure depends mainly upon themselves.

3) The Anxiety Type

Those who are profoundly convinced that the great majority of marriages are doomed to failure from the outset are really expressing their own fears. They lack confidence in their ability to co-operate fully and effectively in the marriage partnership. Possibly a strong sense of inferiority makes them believe that they do not stand so good a chance as other people in most things, and they feel that in so important a matter as marriage they are certain to fail. Or they may recoil emotionally from accepting the responsibilities which marriage entails. They tend to be self-centered, and so find it impossible to enter fully and wholeheartedly into a relationship which is based on the idea of mutual cooperation.

Unhappily, many people see others, possibly those near and dear to them, who fail in marriage. All kinds of people, including those who are very successful in other ways, are found among the marital failures. Many defeatists argue that if intelligent, even brilliant, people fail in marriage; their own chances of success are indeed remote. But this can be said with complete confidence: *If two people bring to marriage reasonable intelligence and abundant good will, and are both fully determined to make a success of their union, their chances are good.* Belief that they can succeed, combined with

Who Should Go On The Journey? 19

determination to do so, is of the utmost importance. It is this positive outlook which is so often lacking, and which accounts for so many marital failures.

Those who feel that the scales are heavily weighted against happiness in marriage always fail to recognize the essential truth that *marriage is what you make it.* Everything depends upon the behavior of the two partners, and this springs, of course, from their individual make-up. It is absolutely essential to have confidence in order to stand a chance of succeeding in any human activity, and this is particularly true of marriage, which is a lifelong test of the best human qualities.

> ...marriage is what you make it.

The Right Outlook

Marriage is the normal state for adult men and women; but not all who are physically prepared for marriage have grown up emotionally. All the emotional states and attitudes which we have just considered are founded on infantile traits of one kind or another. The most important question, therefore, which all who contemplate marriage should ask themselves IS this: AM I SUFFICIENTLY MATURE TO MARRY? This is not just a matter of age. It does not apply only to *young* people who are considering matrimony. There are men and women of fifty whose attitudes are intensely infantile.

Nine out of ten victims of infantile traits are firmly convinced that they are completely normal and that only those who cross their path or interfere with their plans are abnormal I Moreover, it is not always helpful to lay down set rules as a guide to emotional maturity. Some people apply them very strictly to themselves, and others—usually those who are somewhat deficient in adult qualities—tend to rate themselves highly at their weakest points.

Perhaps the best indication as to whether or not you have an adult emotional make-up will be shown by your emotional response to this article. If when you have read it you feel that the demands it makes are grossly unreasonable, and that you can manage your marriage without the bother of seeking adaptation to your partner in all the numerous ways indicated, it is more than probable that you are not emotionally prepared for the serious tasks of marriage. On the other hand, if the suggestions leave you with the impression that marriage is not a simple matter, but a challenge to the best that is in you,

Who Should Go On The Journey? 21

worthy of every possible effort on your part to make it a success, then the chances are that your outlook and attitudes are fairly satisfactory.

Contrary to popular belief, emotional maturity is not a matter of formal education or of general intelligence. Great ability and a wide range of knowledge do not necessarily go hand in hand with such homely but essential virtues as tolerance and kindness. If, being perfectly honest with yourself, you can answer "Yes" to the following questions you are certainly emotionally equipped to assume the responsibilities and to know the joys which marriage can bring.

1. Do I know my future partner?

2. Am I fully prepared to accept my share of responsibility?

3. Can I freely give as well as eagerly take?

4. Is it habitual for me to consider the comfort and feelings of others equally with my own?

5. Do I see my prospective husband or wife as he or she really is, with faults as well as good qualities, failings as well as virtues?

6. Am I—an average human being, with weaknesses and failings—capable of striving so to merge my life with another's as to secure the harmonious development of both lives side by side?

You will learn a great deal about yourself by asking, and trying honestly to answer, these questions. And if some of your replies are not completely satisfactory, remember that nobody enters marriage ideally equipped, since we are all imperfect in some ways. But to recognize our limitations as well as our strength is invaluable. It helps us to see things in the right perspective. It shows us where we should aim for improvement; finally—and this is of great importance—it gives us a goal.

We must look to marriage as a task for two. We must accept the fact that we can, by really trying, so order our lives that two people may benefit and that love may grow stronger year by year. We must believe in ourselves and in our partners. We must be prepared to work unceasingly to make our marriage a beautiful and mutually enriching experience.

If you can do all this, your outlook is exactly right and this book will help you.

THE MEANING OF MARRIAGE

Before two people enter into marriage they must be certain of each other's outlook upon it. As it is, far too many married people reproach their partners in some such form as this: "You never told me that this was your idea of marriage. If I had known, I would never have married you."

Husbands and wives cannot pull together if their aims are divergent. And in so important a matter as marriage it is imperative that both should aim high from the outset. "The utmost for the highest" is a motto which has much to commend it in a relationship which is of paramount importance and which may profoundly affect the lives of others, particularly of any children of the marriage.

Broadly speaking, there must be a common purpose, and this can spring only from some shared faith or philosophy. It is not necessary that the prospective partners should see eye to eye on all religious matters, but they need to share fundamental spiritual and moral values. This will give point and purpose to all that they do.

In marriage, they are embarking upon a quest for a common goal—one which two people may attain by mutual effort, but which they cannot attain separately. They need, therefore, the inspiration which high ideals and a sense of spiritual values can impart, and also an understanding of, an agreement regarding, the framework of marriage. Given these, they can pass on to a consideration of some of the details of how they will build a House of Marriage to conform to their ideals.

True Marriage

Marriage is the union of two people who desire each other, not in the sense of a passing physical embrace, but in the fullest, best, and most lasting sense. They want to live in complete intimacy. Nature prompts them to desire physical intimacy. This by itself, however, is not true marriage, though it may be often repeated. When men and women really care for each other, their love makes them feel the need for each other's hearts and minds as well as bodies. They desire each other's companionship. They need each other's support and encouragement. They want to serve each other. Nothing less than *shared* living is enough.

Each has an essential part to play in this union. Neither can manage without the other. If one partner entertains any foolish illusions of the supremacy of either sex, let these be dismissed at once. The sexes are complementary to each other—and might at times be rather more complimentary, if this basic truth were more widely recognized. Even sexual union in its crudest form as a purely physical activity is impossible without the co-operation of both man and woman.

True marriage is therefore the coming together, in complete union, of two people of opposite sex. They are equal, but different. Each is necessary to the other's well-being. And their union must be of a permanent nature.

That must be their intention from the outset. The various theories which have been advanced from time to time in favor of "trial marriage," "free unions," and the like, are really not theories about marriage itself. They are substitutes for marriage. They are second-best suggestions for those who are incapable of mastering, or too timid to accept, true marriage.

Why Marriage?

Marriage and the family are closely linked and interwoven, and it is through the family and its needs that we can perhaps best appreciate why marriage must be of a permanent character if it is to serve the highest ends. The family is the most fundamental and the most important of all the groups, large or small, in which men and women are associated. And who started it? No statesman issued a decree that from a certain date families should be brought into existence. No moralist hit upon the family idea.

> The family is the most fundamental and the most important of all the groups, large or small, in which men and women are associated.

The family is part of Nature's scheme. Without it the young could not obtain adequate protection and nourishment—including emotional nourishment, which is not less important than food and drink.

This is a very important point to be borne well in mind in connection with marriage, for from it we may learn the vital truth that any relaxation of the marriage bond, which must inevitably tend toward the dissolution of family life, is not only contrary to all the best moral teachings, but is diametrically at variance with Nature's laws.

The Family Triad

Look at it this way. You owe your existence to two people—your father and mother. There you have the oldest society the world has known, the triad of father, mother, and child. You may have to live under a dictatorship which changes all the rules and regulations regarding marriage and the family. You may be foolish and infantile and try to "emancipate" yourself from all "old-fashioned" ideas of marriage and family. But do what you will, the fact remains that on the very day you were born a new society was established— your family.

Much can happen to any family. Its members may be compelled to live apart, even in different parts of the world. But no one can give you any other mother than the mother who bore you. Nothing can give you any other father than the one who begat you.

Think over these things and consider some of their implications. They will help you to realize just why it is so essential that everything to do with marriage and the family should be approached with a high sense of responsibility.

The Meaning Of Marriage 29

Even more significant from this point of view is the undeniable truth that once you were born your father and mother could do nothing to annul the fact of your birth. It was beyond their power to change their relationship to you, or to escape responsibility not merely for your being on this earth but for all the consequences arising from the birth, as the result of their union, of another being.

In very truth you are part of them. In body, mind, emotional make-up, and traditional outlook you have sprung from both of them. You are the living embodiment of their union, though they may have been dead for years. And soon, if you marry, you may be continuing the succession, passing on the same influences, though now merged with others, which once helped to make you what you are.

It is only by taking this realistic view, by considering precisely what the family is and how it concerns us as individuals, that we can see why marriage must be a permanent relationship and not something to be taken up or dropped according to the mood of the moment. Only by frankly facing these inescapable facts of life—for such they are—can we adopt a realistic attitude toward marriage.

Marriage is the mother of the family. And the family is indisputably a permanent society. How, then, can any rational person regard marriage as anything but a permanent relationship—"Till death us do part"? And all the other temporary unions, trial marriages and so forth, are merely unsatisfactory substitutes for the real thing.

Human Love

But the arguments already put forward in support of the view that marriage must be permanent or it is not really marriage are by no means the whole of the case. There are powerful further considerations. One of them is Love.

It is amazing how those who seek to decry marriage and who advocate various alternatives to it invariably make much of love as a justification for their disregard of all laws—human and divine. "If two people love each other, nothing else matters" is the cheap novelette argument of these marriage reformers (re-actionaries would be a more apt description). The truth is that if two people really love each other they invariably want to live the true married life.

> The truth is that if two people really love each other they invariably want to live the true married life.

The Meaning Of Marriage

The "reformers" who pretend to be concerned about lifting human relations to a higher level are really dragging people down to a lower human level. They are calling us back to days when the human race was little, very little, superior to the animal creation. Their whole outlook upon sex and marriage is animalistic. The tragedy is that they can rarely be brought to realize this fact!

The sex act, or physical mating, of men and women differs little if at all from that of animals unless it is prompted and guided by love. Cut out the inspiration of love, and what have you? Simply this: One person using the other, or each using the other, as a thing, a convenience, a mere source of physical gratification,

But what happens if love is present? The relationship is lifted to a higher level and becomes an activity suited to human beings with centuries of experience, progress, and culture behind them. And can this en lightened, matured activity be enjoyed with a dozen or a score of mates?

The answer may be given in the words of the Right Rev. E. J. Hagan: "Is it not of the very essence of genuine natural love to be single-minded and exclusive? The lover desires to possess the beloved for himself and by himself, and the entry of a third party is felt to be an intolerable intrusion. It is not denied that the polygamous instinct does exist, nor that alongside the desire for exclusive possession there exists also an impulse toward variety and change. But this desire for change becomes operative not through the strength, but through the weakness of love. Genuine natural love between man and woman resists change and intrusion, and insists that the tie between them is exclusive and permanent."

This is not a mere theory. It is part of the regular, day-by-day experience of thousands of men and women who love. They feel, while strongly under the influence of love, that they desire nothing more than to be forever faithful to the beloved. And they ask that such faithful devotion as they wish to give shall be accorded to themselves.

This is perfectly reasonable. Men and women who are willing to give all for love are entitled to expect loyalty in return. There is nothing "old-fashioned" or absurd in the idea. It is only fair. And in this perfectly fair, common-sense attitude we find the basis of marriage.

If you intend to marry, it is essential that, from the start, both you and your prospective partner decide whether or not this pledge of mutual loyalty is

The Meaning Of Marriage   33

too much to give. If it means too big a denial, too great a sacrifice, depend upon it you are not ready for marriage. *You do not love enough.*

Many other reasons may occur to you, but that is the real one. For love will make you desire above all to be loyal, and at the same time to expect loyalty.

If you are firmly prepared to vow lifelong loyalty to each other—but not unless—you can consider the various other matters about which agreement in advance is desirable. These are really the plans of two people who are pledged to each other—the ways and means by which they intend to make their shared relationship happy and productive of the best results. We shall consider these in the next topic.

But now, before passing to the planning stage, pause and consider all that has been said in this chap ter. Are you quite certain that both you and your prospective partner understand what marriage entails and are fully prepared to accept its obligations? If you are, that is the best possible start.

You may have to journey far in the quest of the ideal, but every step will be in the right direction.

Your Life Together

PLANNING IN ADVANCE

When two people decide to marry, and are agreed as to what marriage involves, a certain amount of planning is necessary. Usually this does not go far enough. It is very important that plans should be made regarding the general lines of the future relationship and that agreement should be reached between the partners on matters which, otherwise, might yield conflict between them.

First and foremost among these must be placed the financial arrangements. A girl who is asked to marry a man is entitled to know what his earnings are and what are his prospects. If she intends to continue to work after her marriage she should be equally frank regarding her earnings. Marriage is a shared relationship, a partnership; and the income which supports this partnership should be regarded as a joint one.

Planning In Advance

It is not possible to lay down any hard-and-fast rules, because individual circumstances vary greatly. But it is a sound general principle to regard all money earned by either of the partners as representing joint income out of which all expenses must be paid, and the balance shared.

Nothing is more galling to a young woman who may have earned a good wage prior to marriage than to have to ask her husband for every penny she requires for her personal use. There are wives of well-to-do husbands who never have any money to call their own. A fixed, rigid housekeeping allowance is allotted to them, but nothing more.

Men who act in this way have usually contrived to persuade themselves that women cannot be trusted to manage money wisely and well. Actually, nothing annoys them more than that a woman should prove to be a sound money-manager. For such men are really compensating for their feelings of inadequacy and inferiority by keeping a woman dependent upon themselves. The childish desire to have someone dependent, in one's power, can wreak havoc in marriage.

Consideration of family finances should not only include the basic question of how the income is to be apportioned as between the partners. It is very necessary to prepare for the proverbial "rainy day." However small the family income may be, it is desirable that something should be saved regularly, week by week or month by month.

Many young husbands take out life-insurance policies so that, in case of death, their wives will be provided for.

It is not suggested that a policy for any specific amount should be taken out. Attention is directed to this matter because, with life insurance, the earlier one takes out a policy the smaller are the premiums. Moreover, one may not be in a position to insure, at any rate so favorably, when older, for the state of one's health has to be taken into consideration.

The attitude which insists upon complete control of the purse strings inevitably finds expression in other spheres as well. Some men assume that, because they are the "breadwinners," they are entitled not only to decide how the family income shall be apportioned (which usually means that the wife has a very thin time financially) but that they alone must decide how the home shall be run, when holidays shall be taken, and indeed almost everything else.

It is such things as these which often produce a great strain upon the partners. They should be dis-

Planning In Advance

cussed in advance of marriage. What type of home is to be established after marriage? What shall be done in the way of entertaining? How shall the home be run? Will housekeeping duties be shared to some extent, and if so, how? What is to be the attitude to in-laws? Shall visits by both the husband's and wife's relations be encouraged, or not? What religious observances shall be followed, and in what faith, in the case of a mixed marriage, shall any children of the union be brought up?

One matter regarding which difficulties sometimes arise is that of holidays.

Whether or not holidays should be spent together is entirely a matter of choice on the partners' part, but it is very desirable that agreement should be reached on this question. Some very happily married people regularly take their holidays separately and thoroughly enjoy hearing each other's accounts of how they have fared. Others find the very idea of spending holidays apart from each other quite unthinkable.

> ... always bear well in mind that one of the deadly enemies of marriage is boredom.

When planning ahead, always bear well in mind that one of the deadly enemies of marriage is boredom. The young girl who loves her fiancé dearly may find it hard to believe that life could be dull so long as she shared the same home with him. But if he is very keen on cards and enjoys playing evening after evening, she will suffer agonies of boredom unless she happens to share his enthusiasm.

In order to plan ahead wisely and well you must consider your own inclinations and also those of your prospective partner. Both matter. It is a great mistake to assume that because you love a person you should submit to a life which is boring or even repugnant to you. That can only lead, sooner or later, to trouble.

All the matters so far mentioned in this chapter should come under consideration prior to marriage, as well as others which affect your own particular case. And in considering them, bear constantly in mind that, if things go well, your married life will last for a long time. It is necessary to remind yourself that, although at present you may be "wrapped up in each other," friends and relations must inevitably form an essential background to your living and loving.

The young couple who overlook this may find, later in life that they have drifted apart from those hitherto nearest to them. That can be a tragedy. While it is right and necessary that, during the first year or

Planning In Advance

two, a young married couple should spend most of their time together, with as little interruption of their shared living as possible, only harm can result from rigidly excluding friends and relatives.

While it is impossible to list all the items which require consideration before marriage, since individual circumstances and inclinations vary so much, two exceptionally important subjects should be thrashed out very thoroughly in every case. One of them has already been touched upon—family finances. The other concerns children.

The experience of married people generally is that children are among the greatest blessings which life can offer. Certainly those who reach middle life with out having children, either because they deliberately avoided doing so or because they were unable to have them, invariably lament their childless state.

Marriage without children seems incomplete. Many factors affect the question of how many children are desirable, and it is impossible to give advice likely to be helpful in every case. But one safe rule can be confidently recommended:

Always discuss the question of children before marriage and plan for the first three years of married life. It need hardly be said that whatever plans are agreed upon may not be rigidly adhered to. Circumstances may change. What may seem out of the question prior to marriage may become possible of attainment later. But where this is so, the change of policy should result from discussion. By starting along the lines of discussion and joint planning, and continuing in that way, many of the difficulties which often trouble married couples will be avoided.

Finally, if one of the prospective partners holds strong views on religion and the other does not or holds different views, it is very necessary to decide in advance what shall be the joint attitude toward this subject. In so essentially a personal matter as religion it is often best to provide the fullest opportunity for religious observance to the partner who feels drawn to this. There must be no joking at his or her expense. Each must respect the other's conviction, even if unable to share it.

Bear well in mind, also, that the guidance and solace which religion can provide may contribute much toward making and keeping your home and family life the beautiful and ennobling influence you would wish it to be.

THE TWO TRAVELERS

Marriage involves a lifelong journey with your partner as traveling companion. It is desirable, therefore, to know something of the differences between the sexes.

A man can look at a woman and a woman can look at a man; each can observe differences of physical make-up. But what matters most cannot be noted so easily. The way men and women look at things, their outlook and their attitudes, are of primary importance. Unless mental and emotional differences between the sexes are understood both men and women invariably endow their partners with their own characteristics. They judge them by their own standards. This can lead to disagreements and misunderstandings.

Many a couple find themselves faced with some little difficulty because they do not see "eye to eye" in some matter. The husband honestly determined to be fair and reasonable, repeatedly presents to his wife a closely reasoned case. But reason as he will, he fails to make any impression. His wife remains adamant, if instinctively she feels he is wrong.

Feminine Intuition

In the living of their lives women are largely guided by an intuitive sense. Men generally tend to adopt a more "rational" attitude. They usually pride themselves upon this. But it must be confessed that masculine decisions are not generally sounder than intuitive feminine ones. He would indeed be a bold man who would maintain that women's decisions, taken as a whole, were not so satisfactory, if not more so, than men's. The innumerable happy decisions made by mothers are rarely reasoned out, they spring from an understanding of what is best for the family, and they are usually sound.

The man who enters marriage with a full appreciation of the value of woman's intuitive judgment is fortunate.

Nature has endowed woman with this fundamental instinct. A woman's highly emotional make-up is part of her equipment for motherhood. It explains her almost uncanny ability to make sound decisions, particularly with everything related to motherhood, including the upbringing of a family.

All events connected with this function are inevitably associated with strong emotional feelings in the woman. The date on which her marriage took place, the dates of her children's birthdays, special anniversaries in the family's career—all these are of significance to her. That is why wise husbands are careful to remember such anniversaries, which nearly always mean more to a woman than to a man.

It is essential to remember when inevitable differences of opinion occur that there is a masculine and a feminine way of approaching them. We are not composed, in our emotional make-up, of one hundred per cent masculine or feminine qualities. There is a mixture of both in all of us. If this were not so, the sexes would be unable to understand each other sufficiently to achieve reasonable harmony.

In the main, men tend to look at things in a masculine manner and women in a feminine manner. The wife who feels very strongly that her view is sound should adopt a sympathetic attitude toward her husband, who lacks her own intuitive sense and so has to rely upon reason as a guide. His weighing of pros and cons may prove exceedingly irritating to her unless this is recognized. The husband, too, must be wary lest he condemn his wife's habit of "jumping to conclusions," unmindful of the fact that she does so as a result of her intuitive sense.

The Mother Instinct

The main difference between the sexes arises from woman's possession of the maternal instinct. There is no corresponding paternal instinct. True, the term is sometimes loosely used to denote those feelings of fatherly affection and family pride which most men acquire if they have a family. But it is not a deep-rooted, fundamental urge comparable to the maternal instinct which exists in the normal woman.

Very few men realize how strong this instinct is. They do not appreciate that it affects the outlook even of the young, unmarried girl. It is true that the instinct does not reveal itself fully until the role of motherhood is being performed.

The very fact that she is prepared by Nature to assume the maternal role makes her, to some extent, a mother in outlook. She tends to assume a protective attitude toward her child, even though that child is as yet unborn. Without being aware of the fact, she is expressing her maternal instinct when, strongly urged by her young man to agree to pre-marital sexual intercourse, she firmly insists upon waiting until after marriage. She may feel a strong urge to mate physically; but always, with her, the long-term aspect takes precedence over the short-term. She looks ahead. Her needs can be met only by conditions which give the children a good chance to survive and live happily. That is why marriage is essential to the sexual expression of the normal woman.

On the other hand, the young man may secure immediate physical gratification from an act of physical union and then turn his mind to other things, little affected by what has occurred. It may seem to him absurd that the girl should attach so much impor-tance to being married before union is affected, par-ticularly if both parties are fully determined to marry eventually.

If the maternal instinct is fully aroused as the result of pre-marital intercourse, the results may be far-reaching. A young man may be astonished that a single act of union should seem to the girl involved to bind him to her forever. He may feel that she is extremely foolish and unreasonable to

The Two Travelers

attach so much importance to what appears to him no more than an incident. It is very necessary that young people should know that, for women, the sex act carries with it a part of the expression of the maternal instinct. All that is involved in preparing for the child, its birth and subsequent upbringing, are included in her sexual expression. Once this powerful, fundamental instinct has been fully aroused it demands expression in many ways. In marriage it affects all relations with the husband and every activity connected with the home and the upbringing of children.

It follows that women are extremely sensitive to interference in what they rightly regard as their special sphere, the one for which Nature has given them qualifications far superior to any possessed by men. But they are also extremely gratified by friendly, genuine cooperation.

The man who understands women will never make the mistake of assuming that he knows better than his wife what to do regarding the children or their upbringing. On the other hand, he will not act as though the home and the children were no concern of his. He will realize that, no matter how good a husband and father he may be, he can never play so important a part as his wife in the lives of the children, especially during the vital early years when the child's life patterns are formed. The father may be the head of the family, but the mother is the heart of it.

The Fundamental Difference

This brings us to the fundamental difference in outlooks and attitudes. Because of her essential role, because she is endowed by Nature for motherhood, woman possesses a greater degree of emotional maturity than man.

This truth—surprising, even startling, though it may seem to some—can be easily verified. Is not the girl of twenty invariably more "grown up," more adult in outlook and attitude than the youth of twenty? Women not only attain emotional maturity more quickly than men; they achieve a higher degree of emotional security and confidence.

One can see the hand of Nature in this. It is because she possesses this greater degree of emotional security that a woman assumes the responsibilities of motherhood and of family upbringing. But it is because he is driven by a fundamental insecurity and inferiority that the man feels the urge to go out into the world and strive to achieve success, thereby providing for the family's material needs.

The Two Travelers

It is perfectly true that, unfortunately, many women suffer from uncertainty because of economic circumstances which undermine the underlying sense of security which surrounds the performance of the mother role. But give to any mature woman a reasonably comfortable home and a sufficient income to maintain it, and she will find her happiness there.

Not only does the different degree of emotional maturity achieved by the marriage partners affect their attitude to the outside world, it also affects their relationship to each other.

The wife is constantly performing a maternal role toward her husband, even though she may be quite unconscious of that fact. She is led by her own nature to "mother" him in many ways. And the man, much more the victim than the woman of infantile traits, seeks a mother who will comfort and encourage him. In other words, whereas girls grow up to be mothers, even to their husbands, boys never entirely leave the baby or little-boy stage so far as emotional development is concerned.

If, from the outset, these fundamental differences between the sexes are recognized, both husband and wife will find it much easier to understand each other, and indeed themselves.

The question is often asked: How is it that so many people who have had little education and know nothing of the workings of the mind succeed in achieving a happy marriage? The answer is that Nature has taught them all that matters. It is those who fail, in some respects, to perform the task allotted to them by Nature who turns to the psychologist for aid in diagnosing their troubles and affecting a cure.

Certainly the happiest women have never found the secret of their happiness in books or lectures. They do the right thing instinctively.

As for men, because they are emotionally immature in comparison with women, they tend to seek a mother in their wives, as we have noted. But they cannot have it both ways. If they feel the need, as most men do, of almost "motherly" solace and encouragement from their wives, they must realize some of the implications of this emotional relationship. By all means let them strive for success in the outside world. By all means let them feed their confidence— which often sorely needs nourishment!—by a little harmless boasting if success comes their way. But in the home they cannot be both Big Boss and Big Baby. Far too many men try to perform both roles and wonder why they fail.

The Two Travelers

Not only do the two travelers need to know something of the differences of outlook which characterize the sexes. It is also important that they should observe well the individual attitudes which exist in men and women alike, and see how they may harmonize them as between themselves.

Background Differences

One difficulty in this connection lies in ascertaining the prospective partner's real attitude as distinct from the surface, or apparent, attitude. Two young people met at a Left Wing political discussion group. They both abhorred class distinctions. They seemed to have everything in common. When they decided to marry, even expert observers might have been forgiven for assuming that here was a union almost certain to prove successful.

For some reason or other, the girl had always felt scornful of what she called "the City clerk type." If she saw black-coated, bowler-hatted men hurrying for a train she would say: "Look at them—the world's worms, a lot of mental navvies." She could not explain this utterly absurd dislike of a group of men who obviously include many different types, but there it was.

Her husband, whom prior to marriage she invariably saw when dressed for leisure activities, was a bank clerk. After marriage, she felt she could scream each time she saw him arrayed in black coat and striped trousers, and hurrying to join the others who caught the 8:30 every morning.

We all have our likes and dislikes. It is only when they are intense that they are really dangerous to happy human, and therefore, marriage, relationships. But the example given illustrates the kind of attitude which may go far toward ruining a marriage. It is necessary that all who contemplate marriage should, be aware of any strong aversions in themselves and in their partners, and should consider carefully whether these will prove hindrances to mutual adjustment.

Living Standards

One offshoot of the romantic illusion which has been fostered in fiction and plays concerns the economic aspect of marriage. The idea is that if people really love each other they will be happy, even though one of the partners has left luxurious life in a castle for plain living in a cottage. It is true that examples exist of those who have been accustomed to every luxury yet have adapted themselves to a

The Two Travelers

much lower living standard after marriage and have been happy, but this does not mean that a lowered living standard is of little importance. It may make a very big difference.

The mere fact that one of the partners has, prior to marriage, lived at, say, a $1000-a-year rate and after marriage has to manage on $400 a year is not of itself as significant as the attitude toward life of the individual concerned. If he or she likes good clothes and expensive entertainments, and all the other things which can be enjoyed by those with ample means, obviously any serious reduction in living standards will create difficulties. On the other hand, some who have been accustomed to every advantage which money can buy actually prefer to live simply and inexpensively.

A young man with a steady job who is unlikely ever to earn more than enough to keep a family supplied with minimum requirements may intend to marry the daughter of a fellow employee. But the fact that the economic level of the two families is similar is not sufficient. What of their inclinations and tastes?

The girl works in a dress shop. She likes her work. She has a liking for good clothes although she cannot afford to spend too much. There may be other directions—there probably are—in which she has tastes which, while not in any sense extravagant, nevertheless make her tend to think and act along rather more expensive lines than those involved where the one aim is to keep expenditure down to the absolute minimum. She may not be able to afford to visit the theater frequently, but she likes to go when she can, and to have a good seat. In fact, she would much prefer to go once a year and see a really good play or opera in comfort than visit the movies or occupy a gallery seat at the theater once a week.

If marriage means the loss of much that has hitherto made life enjoyable, it starts under a disadvantage, and as the years pass the strain may become intolerable.

The young man who is eager to marry may deceive himself as to the cost of maintaining a home. He may tend to overlook the fact that some of his habits are firmly established and that after marriage he cannot possibly afford to live in the style to which he has been accustomed. All this may seem obvious when we consider the more extreme examples. It is more likely to be overlooked when it concerns only such ordinary, everyday matters as expenditure upon drink, tobacco, or sport. When marriage involves relinquishment of the kind of life you like, unless you are careful you may soon find it irksome. Such

> **It takes two people to make a marriage– and two happy people to make a happy marriage.**

things as these rarely receive sufficient consideration prior to marriage, yet often they are powerful contributory factors toward marital unhappiness. It is very easy to deceive oneself regarding them.

The great essential to bear in mind is that, before marriage, you should learn as much as possible regarding the man or woman you contemplate marrying. And you should consider carefully how his or her attitude fits in with yours. *For it takes two people to make a marriage—and two happy people to make a happy marriage.*

THE FIRST
TWO YEARS

The start of any journey is important. A good start sets the course in the right direction. It puts the travelers in good heart. They feel that they are making progress. They therefore gain confidence in themselves and in each other.

So far as marriage is concerned, it is best to regard the first two years as the first phase. It is true that most people look upon the honeymoon as the start of the journey, and some writers have given to this brief holiday—for such it really is—a significance far beyond its real importance.

Thus it is sometimes said that marriages are either made or marred on the honeymoon—an exaggeration, but containing at least a grain of truth. All that happens on the honeymoon is important. But it is only of exceptional importance because it occurs *right at the start* of the marriage journey. It would be just as important if the couple did not go away on a

The First Two Years　　　　　　　　　　　　　　　61

honeymoon, but began their married life at home, living from the start in the conditions in which their shared relationship would continue.

I sometimes think that it would be a good thing if people who intend to marry were to ask themselves, and each other, the question: *Is our honeymoon really necessary?*

This may seem a startling question to some. But it is one which is worthy of careful consideration, since there is much to be said both for and against the honeymoon custom.

Honeymoon: For and Against

Those who feel that the very idea of marriage without a honeymoon at the outset is quite unthinkable might ponder upon this quotation from *A Short History of Marriage,* by Ethel L. Urlin:

"The honeymoon is a relic from the old days of marriage by capture. Far from being a pleasure trip, as it is now, it was a hurried flight made necessary by the almost certain wrath of the bride's father. For at least a month the audacious pair kept out of his way, and at the end of that time strove to reconcile him to the situation by making him handsome presents."

So it seems that unless the newly married couples have good reason to fear the bride's father, there is no reason at all why they should go to the expense of a honeymoon, just at the time when money is most needed.

If the honeymoon were always a help, no one would think of questioning its worth. There is something to be said for a short holiday during which the partners are freed from all distractions and can get to know each other more thoroughly and intimately than has hitherto been possible, or permissible. But far too often it proves a hindrance, since it involves the marriage starting under conditions which are to some extent unreal.

After all, the true test of marriage is not how well two people can get along together for a week or two when they are free to concentrate entirely upon each other, it is how they can manage, year in and year out, when dealing with all the innumerable problems and practical affairs of day-by-day living.

So much emphasis has been placed upon the importance of the honeymoon that many people regard it as something of vital significance which must on no account be missed. It can safely be said that such an attitude is completely erroneous. It is dangerous, too, for it causes people to attach far too much importance to what is, when all is said and done, nothing more than a holiday.

If we look upon the honeymoon simply as a holiday, then there is much to be said in favor of deferring it and having an extra good holiday together at the most convenient time.

Old customs die hard, and no suggestions of mine are likely to cause any considerable number of readers to forgo the honeymoon. Of that I am aware. So let me utter a few words of warning regarding some of the misleading ideas which are widely held on this subject.

The Right Attitude

First, bear well in mind the fact—for fact it is—that compared with normal married life, the honeymoon is merely a playtime. The serious business of living together comes later. It is then that the real test begins.

It is not surprising that many find their honeymoons delightful in almost every respect. The conditions are entirely favorable, which is rarely the case in ordinary, everyday life. And many husbands and wives look back at the happy days of the honeymoon and sigh for their return. They compare their feelings when facing the humdrum daily round with the joys they experienced on their honeymoon. They feel cheated, and blame their marriage or their partners, failing to realize that the conditions are totally different.

A sound recognition of the real nature of the honeymoon will enable those who sigh for the return of honeymoon joys to realize that they are simply longing for a holiday together in which they can be absorbed in each other just as they were during the honeymoon. Well, there is nothing to prevent them doing this, unless they have ceased to take as much interest in each other as they once did!

Do not expect everything to go exactly right during the honeymoon. While it is true that the background factors are usually favorable, the fact remains that you are both novices in marriage, and most of the necessary knowledge—indeed, the most important part of it—can be acquired only through actual experience of the marriage which has only just begun.

One result of the romantic view of the honeymoon is that some people expect far too much of this short holiday. They should remember that there are years of shared living ahead. These should bring much joy. It is foolish to expect it all at once.

Making a Sound Start

Whether you go on a honeymoon or not, patience and tact must be exercised by both partners during the early days of marriage, and particularly upon the wedding night. Many of the difficulties which are experienced at this time are not really the responsibility of the partners; they arise from faulty upbringing. Where a faulty outlook on sex has been inculcated in childhood, this inevitably affects the first physical embraces and may produce disharmony right at the start.

If you recognize this fully, it will prove a great aid. It will help you to act wisely. We all have inhibitions of various kinds and of varying degree. It is therefore particularly necessary to go slowly during the early days of marriage. No bigger mistake could be made than to act as though the whole future success of your marriage depends upon your indulging to the full in the physical embrace at this time.

Because sex has been treated in books, plays, and lectures as though it were something apart from life, instead of being an essential part of total living, most of us experience a good deal of anxiety, fear, or shame—or possibly all of these—in connection with sexual expression. What should be approached in a spirit of keen anticipation, and participated in with happy abandon, may seem surrounded with difficulties and fraught with dangers.

This is widely recognized, but many people make the mistake of supposing that the remedy lies in a bold, heavy frontal attack, as though the inhibitions and faulty attitudes of years could be banished in an hour or a day. It is far better to "hasten slowly."

Because of the emotional make-up of most women, the wedding night is of exceptional significance to them. Nothing which happens then is trifling. This presents dangers, but it also offers opportunities. The wise handling of the problems associated with the first intimate relations can powerfully contribute to the establishment of mutual trust and understanding.

There can be no doubt that one of the most dangerous enemies of harmony in the early intimate contacts is undue prominence of the masculine element. Sexologists have tended, in recent years, to write and speak almost entirely from a masculine viewpoint, and have therefore underrated the importance of the feminine contribution. They have said, with truth, that the bride is rarely able to experience full enjoyment of the intimate embrace, and have concentrated upon counseling

The First Two Years

thoroughness of preparation on the man's part—more love-play, kisses, caresses, before the act of union. But this does not go far enough. We need to recognize that in these early days we have to act in accordance with the woman's tempo. The more so if as a result of upbringing she is unduly inhibited in this regard. The fundamental outlook on marriage should always be a long-term one, and for this, if for no other reason, the keynote on the man's part should be—patience.

> ... the keynote on the man's part should be patience.

The Real Test

The real test comes when, having lived together through all the excitement of courtship, honeymoon, and first embraces; the partners have to adjust themselves to everyday life. It is then that the husband's emotional inadequacy is usually painfully apparent.

As we have seen, the woman's basic outlook is firmly founded on her maternal instinct, and this equips her mentally and emotionally for her task. But the husband is not so equipped for his part. On the contrary, his life has hitherto been lived along lines not conducive to marriage.

Whereas the wife has really only one *basic* problem to solve—how to adjust herself to her husband—he has two. He not only has to learn adjustment to his wife, but—and this may prove more difficult—he has to attain adjustment to the new conditions of living.

I regard the first two years of married life as the critical period, for much depends upon the measure of "re-education" attained by the husband during this time. If two years seems too long to allow for a husband to achieve adaptation to living the married life, just think precisely what is involved.

Not only is he endowed, like all men, with a lesser degree of emotional maturity than most women possess—a big handicap in itself!—but all his life has been devoted to pleasing himself, to living (broadly speaking) as though he alone mattered. Very few boys play so active a part in the home as do girls as a matter of course, and when they have performed some little service they have usually felt as though they were being exceedingly good! It is amazing how men give themselves rows of medals for doing for an hour what women do year in and year out. Even when engaged in the task of looking after themselves, most males, irrespective of age, usually rely very largely upon the ministrations of female relatives. The man of thirty who marries has been dependent upon women, to a varying degree, but always to an important extent, all his life; and then, instead of living for himself, he must live for another as well. *He has to learn to share.*

Let it be admitted at once that most men enter marriage fully intending to pull their weight. They feel that they are assuming responsibilities which they did not possess before. They are determined to discharge them. But although the best of intentions are usually present, the fact remains that many men carry into marriage part, at least, of the attitude which has been theirs in the past. Nobody can fling off, at will, the attitudes of years and be done with them in a flash. It means re-educating emotional expression. It involves the best type of self-discipline.

Needless to say, some girls who have been spoiled all their lives bring to marriage the resultant inadequacies. They, too, find it hard, if not impossible, to adapt themselves to the new conditions. But what a commentary upon our methods of upbringing that the overwhelming majority of men have to start re-education regarding the most vital things in life *after they have married!*

And not only does upbringing make it very difficult for men to get accustomed to giving instead of constantly taking, other factors, even customs associated with marriage itself, tend to encourage the husband to take rather than give. These are really surviving traditions from days when female subjection was taken for granted. They make it harder for the husband to shake off his former habits and take on a fresh set.

For instance, while we shout from the housetops that now and henceforth the sexes must be regarded as equal, we still expect a woman to provide a trousseau, whereas the man is not called upon to do anything of this kind.

If the idea of absolute equality between the sexes found expression right through our marriage ideas we should not, perhaps, abolish the trousseau, but we should have a husband's trousseau as well as a wife's.

This is, of course, really a minor matter and one upon which we need not dwell beyond pointing out that such things as this—and others could be mentioned—tend to encourage the husband to think of marriage in terms of his own advantage instead of as something which equally affects two people.

Most women find it very much easier to share their lives, simply because they have been

The First Two Years

doing so to some extent long before marriage. It is helpful for them to realize the difficulties which husbands experience in this change-over of habits, for much depends upon their understanding and encouragement.

The upbringing of girls prepares them for marriage to a considerable degree, but while it is helpful for the wife to be ready and even eager to play her part in the shared life, she may need to remind herself that she is an equal in the marriage partnership. Many women have grown so accustomed to the purely domestic role that they overlook their rights in every other sphere. They may even be afraid to ask for things they really need, or at any rate refrain from doing so until they can contain themselves no longer and then indulge in an angry outburst.

I have said that it takes two years for most men to adjust themselves to shared living. What of the woman who, prior to marriage, has followed a career? She, too, will not find it at all easy to accept the changed conditions. Working in the home, instead of going out to meet other people in fresh surroundings, may at first seem dull.

When the husband returns from work he may be in need of rest, whereas she is in need of change and active recreation. It is very important that the husband should realize that his wife would welcome an evening out and that the wife should recognize that her husband feels just as keen on an evening at home.

Obviously, both cannot have their way all the time. Apply, then, the principle of sharing. The husband who, although he would like to put his feet up and take things easy at home, takes his wife out in order to meet her wishes will generally find that the little outing will do him good. The wife who stays in to please her husband will enjoy the knowledge that he likes nothing better than the home over which she presides, especially if she knows that the following evening he will take her out. Give and take all the time must be the rule, and you will find in practice that the happiest times for you are those when you are giving and not merely taking. Some find this hard to believe, but it is true.

> Give and take all the time must be the rule, and you will find in practice that the happiest times for you are those when you are giving and not merely taking.

Smoothing Life's Rough Edges

The happy married people are those who, during the early years of marriage, formed sound habits designed to promote mutual happiness. If you start by always staying in, the habit will grow until it becomes difficult to force yourselves to go out. If you never invite people to visit you in your home, you will eventually lead lonely lives. So start right. Form sound habits. For example, one sometimes meets the docile, submissive type of wife who is pathetically anxious to grant every request her husband makes. Almost invariably, neither she nor her husband is happy. Why should men always get their own way? It is not good for them. The wife who enters marriage determined to play her part to insure the success of the relationship will never permit herself to become a doormat provided she understands men. And the chief thing she needs to know about them is that they are emotionally immature. That is why the happiest wives invariably treat their husbands rather like children —without letting their husbands realize that they are doing so!

In a partnership for two there cannot be two bosses. Someone has to take the lead or indecision results. If both partners are genuinely striving to further the welfare and happiness of the other, the problem of leadership invariably solves itself. In some matters, the wife takes the lead. In others, the husband. It is impossible to lay down hard-and-fast rules in this, as everything depends upon the individuals concerned.

But of course it must always be remembered that the marriage partnership, while based on the idea of equality, must also be inspired by love and mutual consideration. Where this is so, leadership comes naturally when needed, and it is not disputed by the other partner in childish fashion—"I'm just as good as you, so why shouldn't I decide?"

I have been profoundly shocked by the manner in which some modern young people apply their strongly held views about equality of the sexes. They assume that this involves being absolutely blunt in their conversation, and it is hardly surprising that the two equals meet in combat very frequently and on the same low level. Absolute frankness is essential to the best results. But frankness does not imply rudeness. What is often called "honesty of expression" is some-times more than a little dishonest.

For instance, if you ask me whether I like your new suit and I reply: "Well, I don't like it at all. It makes you look even more insignificant than usual." I am doing just a little more than asked. You wanted

The First Two Years

an opinion, and I have given it. But I have also added something—worked off a little of my own aggressive feeling, inflicted a little hurt, been thoroughly nasty. I have sought to strengthen my own ego by wounding your self-esteem.

There is far too much of that kind of thing generally. It is rank bad manners. The milk of human kindness is needed even among the best of friends. It is particularly required in marriage.

This extreme "honesty," often taking the form of sheer rudeness, is really a leftover from an earlier period of development. One often observes it in young people who are passing through a difficult emotional phase, but they usually drop it round the age of eighteen. The "emancipated" adults who glory in their extreme bluntness of expression are really revealing their infantile level of development.

The husband or wife who has a tendency to act in this way will find it a valuable corrective to seek out opportunities to express genuine appreciation. Mere flattery will not do. It will be obviously insincere. But if your partner in marriage has not scores of good points you have chosen badly indeed. Try to show your appreciation of what is good, and then you will be listened to attentively when, still careful not to give offense, you point out things which irritate you.

But, of course, if you are to show appreciation of each other's good points, you must know something of each other's lives. Most wives take a keen interest in their husband's work, but if they fail to do so, it is usually the husband's fault. Some men decline to discuss their work at home, and sooner or later their wives accept this and never inquire about how the husband has fared in factory or office. On the other hand, many a woman who is naturally absorbed in. her domestic work realizes that her husband knows little or nothing of what is involved in it.

Some husbands have not the remotest idea what it is like to prepare meals day after day, all the year round. It is true that the "over-domesticated" husband may prove irritating to many a wife. But every husband should be sufficiently interested in his wife's domestic work to acquire for himself some little knowledge of cooking and other domestic activities. The man who can turn his hand to preparing a meal is not only able to act in emergency, but can readily understand what is involved in a constant round of such duties.

What can be more depressing to any wife who takes a keen interest in her domestic work than the knowledge that her husband regards all such tasks as beneath him? Genuine equality in marriage is not

The First Two Years

so much a matter of rules and regulations, laws and customs, as of the spirit. The spirit of equality yields an outlook which cannot possibly despise, either openly or secretly, any of the tasks which one's partner has to perform.

During the first few years you form habits which will last throughout your marriage. It is as well, therefore, to sow seeds deliberately with an eye to their coming to fruition later on.

Some people make the serious mistake of deferring the real business of shared living for as long as possible—until the arrival of the first child, perhaps. During their early years of marriage they crowd in all the pleasure they can. Possibly the wife continues to work, and most of the family income is spent on amusements. Thus a habit is formed of living in an expensive and unreal manner. And having become accustomed to this kind of life, both partners desire no other. They postpone having children. They are really also postponing marriage in its true sense. They grow to fear having to live the normal married life.

The couples who look ahead strive to acquire habits which will serve them well as the years pass. The real joys of life cost little and they provide their utmost benefit when both share them. The natural recreations—walking, listening to the conversation of friends, reading—may be had for the asking. As for sports, those which are based largely on artificial stimulus do not contribute to the stability of marriage. There may seem little harm in watching a number of dogs chasing a mechanical hare, but if there were no betting, would this spectacle attract you evening after evening to the greyhound track?

But, it may be asked, what harm can there be in greyhound racing provided that both husband and wife are willing to allocate a proportion of the family income to throwing money to the dogs? Here you should bear in mind that the habits you form in your everyday living will not only affect both of you, but also your children. These habits will probably prove lasting. You may feel that it is highly undesirable that your children should be encouraged to form gambling habits. You may do your utmost to persuade them that gambling is foolish, since it involves risking money which someone has had to work hard to earn. But the knowledge that Mummy and Daddy go to the "Dogs" will count for much more in their minds than all the anti-gambling arguments ever uttered.

Likewise it is a thoroughly bad sign when married people regard the movies as their main form of recreation, so that if for some reason or other

The First Two Years

they are unable to visit the "pictures" once or twice a week, according to the habit they have formed, their life seems entirely out of joint. The commercialized forms of recreation are highly standardized. They make little or no allowance for individuality. Their patrons tend to acquire one way of looking at things—and that usually, not by any means the best way.

This particularly applies, perhaps, to the movies, which nowadays exerts a tremendous influence over people's lives. It enables day-dreamers to indulge in their weakness, guided by film stars into whose shoes they step for a couple of hours. This kind of escape from reality is harmless enough in small doses. But it often becomes a habit. It grows on some people to an amazing extent. There are movie addicts who are as much in the grip of the silver screen as drug addicts are held in captivity by the drug which has mastered them. Here again is a habit which is better not formed. Far more people patronize the movies than the total of those who engage in all forms of sport and outdoor recreations. They simply sit and watch. They stop living for two hours or more and let others live for them.

Far better to cultivate shared interests which involve active participation. And if there is no recreation which appeals to both partners, then let the sharing principle apply to the manner in which each follows his or her preference. If each Saturday afternoon during the winter the husband is going to enjoy the excitement of a fast game of football, then let him see to it that his wife, too, spends some time, outside of the home, in a pursuit which appeals to her.

Finally, if during the first few years the kind of mutual understanding and adjustment described in this chapter has not been achieved, if unhelpful habits have been formed, then set to work immediately to put things right. This may not be easy. But it can be tackled with a much greater chance of success now than later.

If two people marry and genuinely strive to be the best of companions to each other, thinking first of their own responsibility and not of their individual interests or desires they will almost certainly achieve a happy marriage. If, on the other hand, each considers his or her own interests almost exclusively, then it is practically certain that the marriage will prove a failure.

That is why the first few years are so important. They are the time of opportunity in marriage, and if that opportunity is not wasted, the succeeding years pay rich dividends of happiness and contentment.

THE LOVE
RELATIONSHIP

Marriage is unlike other shared relationships since it includes living in physical intimacy. The fact that it includes this intimate part of the shared life must not cause us to assume, as some unfortunately do, that the success or failure of a marriage is mainly dependent upon the sexual side.

There are many married couples who live very happy lives in which sex, as the term is usually employed, plays very little part.

Sex and Living

There is only one sound and realistic way to regard sex. That is as *a part of total living.* It is an essential part. You cannot altogether escape from it, even if you are foolish enough to try. It is there, and you must accept its presence or else deceive yourself and suffer accordingly.

The Love Relationship   83

Immediately we begin to look upon sex as a part of total living we begin to get things in their true perspective. Instead of trying for all we are worth to insure that we are "good lovers" in the narrow, restricted sense of being capable of arousing and satisfying physical passion, we recognize that the best technique in the world will prove worse than useless *unless the remainder of life's activities are satisfactorily carried out.*

During the last thirty to forty years or so there have been many books dealing with the physical side of sex. These have been helpful to many people. But we must not overlook the fact that thousands of people have lived happy married lives in which sex has played its due part without their having read or been told anything about sex technique. How have they managed? How have they attained genuine adjustment to each other in days when there was no sex instructions, no sex books or other guidance available?

The answer can be given in one word: **Love**.

For the truth is that the best guide to action in the intimate sphere is, and always has been, and forever will be, love—and the tolerance and understanding which are inseparable from it. Love guides us to wise action better than any book possibly can. And love is not limited in its applications. It is not restricted to sex. It affects every aspect of life, beautifies everything it touches, inspires to right action, and calls forth responses of the right kind. No wonder Henry Drummond called his book about love *The Greatest Thing in the World.* For that is love. And if it is the greatest force in your marriage, you have the most precious asset which any married couple could possess.

Love is the one really transforming influence in life. It is the only power which really can change people's lives in a miraculous manner. But we must be clear in our minds as to what we mean by love, for the term is loosely applied to many different emotions. Thus sometimes we hear references made to "selfish love." There can be no such thing.

> Love is the one really transforming influence in life.

Sex and Loving

The one characteristic which must be present where love is, and the one which best enables us to identify love itself, is unselfishness. Many a frail mortal, whose capacity for love is not large enough

The Love Relationship

to enable him to open his heart to the world with all its need, nevertheless feels love toward one person. And where that feeling is directed toward someone of the opposite sex and is accompanied by a desire for union with that person we have the love which provides the soundest possible basis for marriage. There must always be a certain sacrificial quality about love—a willingness to sink individual interests in order to serve a wider unity. And in the married relationship which is founded on love, all that is given up in this way is invariably more than repaid. What each individual partner relinquishes is merged with the sacrifices of the other. The marriage group, and later the family, benefits accordingly.

Does this appear to be platitudinous—remote from the practical aspect which really interests you? Actually it goes to the very heart of the matter when regarded from a realistic point of view. Love is the one essential, and where it is present the physical union, management of the family finances, sharing of responsibilities, duties, and privileges, policy regarding the birth of children, and every other practical activity is influenced and profoundly affected.

We have seen that sex is but a part of total living. As such we all possess it, and must use or misuse it in some way or other. But there is one safe way in which we can use it—as a part of loving. The great essential to success in the sphere of sex relations is that all sexual activity should be inspired, prompted, and guided by love.

What difference does the presence of love make? That is the question which many ask and often they only learn the correct answer when it is too late to benefit them. Without love, sexual activity is often pleasurable. Nature has arranged it thus in order to secure the continuation of the race. But satiety is soon reached where the sex act is performed merely in order to achieve physical gratification. The relief of physical tension may be achieved with various partners and there may not be the slightest inclination even to see any one of them again. But where sex activity is part of loving there is invariably a gradual intensification of the pleasure derived from the relationship—not all of it physical, by any means. There are many married couples whose living and loving has brought constant fresh joys and new happy discoveries. Even in the later years of life the adventure has continued, and new sources of happiness have been found.

Sex as a part of love's expression is the normal and sound way for civilized men and women. It is infinitely superior to the attitude which keeps sex on a purely physical level. But you may realize this to be true yet wonder what any human being can do in order to maintain and develop love. You may doubt whether love can last, save perhaps in the case of a few very fortunate people.

Making Love Last

One of the ailments afflicting humanity today and the root cause of many other troubles is a fatalistic attitude toward life. If someone could inculcate hope into people it would do more good than all the medicine in the world. The fatalistic outlook embraces love. This is seen as something which happens to people for no apparent reason, "comes into their lives," and as suddenly departs. Far too few realize that love is something to be nourished and developed. It can be done, and must be done, by those who would make their marriage successful.

Let us see how it works out in practice. Two modern young people marry. They have discussed sex and have read books about it. They know what the best advisers have to teach so far as sexual activity is concerned. They are mutually attracted to each other. They ought to succeed.

But they fail from the outset. They decide to get the utmost fun out of their honeymoon, and so spend it in, say, Paris. They arrive there tired and hungry, and devote most of each day to sight-seeing and half the night to cabarets. Then they sleep in order to prepare for a fresh day's feverish activities.

This kind of life continues year after year. Curiously enough, their very efficient love-making occupies even less time during the second year than it did during the first, and by the end of the third year they hardly ever embrace except when under the stimulus of alcohol. Before the fourth year has ended they decide they cannot bear the sight of each other and go their separate ways.

Generally, when this kind of thing occurs, the couple either blames each other, or else come to the conclusion that their marriage was a mistake. But, in fact, there was no definite reason for not marrying, and many good reasons why they should have done so. The great mistake they both made from the outset was this: They crowded love out of their lives. They did not sufficiently nourish it. They did not provide the space for it to flourish and expand. Their lives were so full of other things that they had little time for love.

Things might have been different had they planned more wisely, intent above all else upon insuring conditions in which their love could grow. First, they would have realized that during the

The Love Relationship   89

honeymoon the great attraction should have been each other. They should have sought some quiet place where their earliest intimacies could have been enjoyed to the full without interruptions and without unnecessary counter-attractions. As it was, they began their married life with a round of pleasures but without those precious hours of undisturbed mutual revelation and experiment which help so much.

As so often happens, they continued as they began. And the same is true of many people who do not recognize, before they marry, that love is something which needs tending. But how?

Love in Action

It is not very helpful to draw up a list of rules, since so much depends upon the emotional make-up of the two partners in any marriage. But one way of expressing the right attitude to adopt is this:

Let the love relationship rule the whole of your life, occupying all the waking hours and not being confined to specific times or places.

This may seem rather startling at first thought, and for that very reason may stay in the mind. The point is that if love dominates all your activities the sex act will not be merely a physical contact lasting for only a few minutes but the natural and inevitable expression of the fuller love relationship which exists *all the time.* If you can love like that, your marriage will probably prove very happy. If both you and your partner can attain this right relationship to love, then your marriage will be ideally happy.

Sex will assume its rightful place without the slightest anxiety on your part. The urge to the complete physical union may come rarely or often, but whenever it is felt, two people who dearly love each other will use it just as one more means of expressing the love they feel. You will not spend anxious hours wondering whether all is well with your love life. You will probably find it difficult to understand why many people experience "sex difficulties" when this part of your own marriage presents no difficulties and seems perfectly natural— as indeed it should.

The trouble with many people who are over-anxious regarding the sex side of their lives is that they try to follow a routine which they believe is good for themselves or for their partners without realizing

The Love Relationship   91

that different people have different needs in this as in
most other matters. The act of union may occur three
or four times a week with newly married couples and
two or three times a week for those who have been
married for some years. But most couples find that
their needs vary at different times, and it is impossible
to give any useful guidance except:

*Union can be enjoyed—the word is used
deliberately—as often as it is really desired by both
partners provided that there is no artificial stimulation.*

But note the word *desired.* This does not
include the mere observance of a routine habit
into which a couple have fallen. If love is always
the guide, there will be no routine habits in this
sphere. But if the faulty attitude of undue emphasis
on the physical aspect is present, routine will mark
everything you do —including, possibly, a slavish
routine of variety seeking! This can become the
most deadly and monotonous routine of all, whereas
the following of love's promptings insures for most
people ample variety of sexual expression without the
slightest danger of satiety.

Needless to say, love must never be made
the excuse for conduct which is recognized as
undesirable or which is repugnant to the beloved.
Love is often put forward as an excuse for license.

But genuine love is always seeking for opportunities to give rather than to receive, to impart pleasure rather than to secure it. Thus it provides the best kind of safeguard a check or restraining influence from within. This is always preferable to any supervision from without. We are all free, entirely free, to accept love's guidance or to reject it.

Now let us consider what difference the inspiration of love makes to the sex act itself. Love prompts us not to consider ourselves alone, but to seek to impart the utmost pleasure to our partner. The husband who makes himself the willing servant of love does not, therefore, seek to secure his own gratification in the quickest possible time and without regard to his wife's feelings. He desires to show her how much she means to him and to evoke emotional responses in her which will cause a desire for closer union.

Love, the Teacher

This is what is known as love-play. The sex books invariably describe this in some detail and mention how important it is that there should be adequate love-play so as to prepare the wife for the sex act itself. Another point to which attention is usually directed is the need for after-play—that

The Love Relationship 93

is, for spoken endearments and caresses after the culmination of the sex act. There is no need to go into detail here as to the reason why preliminary love-play is important or to describe precisely the physical and emotional responses which it produces. But two things must be noted. These responses may not occur, and certainly will not be complete, if love is lacking. And the preliminary love-play, as well as the after-play which should follow the act of union, do not have to be taught to those who are guided by love. They come naturally as part of love's expression. They were employed by married lovers long before sex books drew attention to their importance!

The happy, spontaneous embrace cannot possibly be fully achieved unless both partners are emotionally as well as physically aroused. Love insures that the strongest and best urge, a blending of the emotional, mental, and spiritual with the physical, yields more than bodily union alone. And in such details as those discussed love makes natural and inevitable the right kind of action.

But while love is the best of guides and in many respects a sound teacher, it does not follow that those who love need know nothing about sex. On the contrary, love causes men and women to turn such knowledge to the best possible account. But bear in mind that sex books, simply because they are sex books, deal mainly with the physical aspect of marriage and so sometimes tend to convey the impression that this is of primary importance.

ADDING TO THE PARTY

a family-planning policy which is ideal for one couple may be hopelessly unsuitable for another. It is therefore impossible to lay down hard-and-fast rules which can be generally recommended. Nevertheless, certain guiding principles may be mentioned. These will serve as a rough indication of the lines along which family policy should be framed. But it has to be recognized that strict adherence to them may be impossible, because individual circumstances vary, ranging from the family's economic position to the emotional makeup of the parents, the mother's health to the living accommodation available, and so on.

Family Building

It will be gathered from this that it is impossible to give an answer to the question which is often asked: *What is the ideal-sized family?* Economists may be able to answer the question from their point of view, and population experts from theirs. A dictator, or a dictatorial government, might determine what size families should be in order to further some national policy. But happily that kind of thing does not happen in a free country. The parents and they alone, are responsible for deciding how many children to have.

The stability of the family and the health and happiness of all its members are the things that matter most. The mother stands out as performing a particularly vital role. Her welfare is of the utmost importance and must be safeguarded above all else. If she suffers in health, or is worn down by strain or too frequent pregnancies, the whole family suffers. With these fundamental considerations as a basis the would-be family planner will find the following four suggestions worthy of careful consideration:

1) *It is generally desirable to aim at having children with an interval of two years between each birth.* This timing is not likely to be rigidly adhered to, but it provides sufficient space between births to give the mother a chance to perform her duties without undue strain and without producing too great a disparity between the ages of the children.

2) *Do not aim at having only one child.* He would lack the friendly rivalry and companionship of brothers and sisters. The full attention of the parents would be concentrated upon him. These and other factors would tend to create emotional difficulties which would affect him not only in childhood, but possibly throughout life.

It is not suggested that the only child inevitably experiences emotional difficulties to a degree which prevents him from living a useful and happy life. This is certainly not the case. But they undoubtedly make his task more difficult than it need be. Both from the parents' standpoint and from that of the child's welfare, an only child is bad policy.

A sound sense of values will help greatly. Children are not to be regarded as a trial, although of course they are bound to be trying at times! They are among life's real gifts, and the home which lacks them is indeed barren.

3) *If possible, have your family before you reach the age of thirty.* There are many reasons for this advice. It is a great advantage both to parents and children for the family to be brought up while the parents are still young. If the births occur when the parents are between the ages of twenty and thirty the relationship may be

more like that of close friends than of parent and child. It is desirable that this advantage of close companionship should be gained. The attitude of the child to his parents, not only during childhood but throughout life, is favorably influenced if the parents are not only kind and attentive, but also good companions.

In this, as in so many important matters in life, it may not be possible to adopt an ideal plan. It must not be assumed that children born of older parents necessarily suffer from marked disadvantages. Generally speaking, it is better for the parents to be under thirty when the children are born, but it doesn't follow that happy, harmonious development is denied to children whose parents are older than this. Often such children enjoy the best of relations with their parents and are very happy.

4) *If there is disagreement regarding family policy, the wife's wishes should prevail.* Occasionally the husband eagerly desires to have a family, but his wife is unwilling, or at least very reluctant. If her husband presses her unduly upon the matter, she may consent. The results are almost invariably unsatisfactory. It is of the utmost importance that no child should be born unless he is desired by his mother.

Welcoming the Newcomer

If the child is to thrive emotionally, he must be welcome from the start, and, indeed, desired before birth.

The child, even in early infancy, knows perfectly well whether or not he is wanted. Long before he knows the meaning of words he can tell if Mother loves him. Her facial expressions, gestures, the tone of her voice and the manner in which she performs the little services which mean so much to the baby, tell him all that he needs to know. Nothing is worse for a child than that he should realize that he is not really wanted, is in the way, and is a burden. This dreadful consciousness, implanted in his mind during infancy, may prejudicially affect his behavior throughout life.

We have noted earlier how important it is that love should be given its rightful place if marriage is to be a happy relationship between the partners. The same applies to the parent-child relationship, and especially to that of the mother and child. Nowadays, when many married women work, there is sometimes

Adding To The Party

a clash of interests, the economic and domestic claims conflicting. It is vital that nothing should stand between the mother and her child, for no one else can give to the child that which he needs most of all if he is to thrive emotionally—the love and tender ministrations of his own mother. There is not the space in which to deal fully with this important matter here, but those who are interested are referred to *Unwanted Child* (Rich and Cowan) by the present author, which deals in detail with this vital social and human problem.

Teaching the Newcomer the Way

When you have children, you will be faced with immense responsibilities. They should be gladly accepted. They provide opportunities for assuring the future happiness of your family and of other families which may spring from it.

Chief among these is that of teaching by practical example *how to live.* For, depend upon it, the child learns more about how to handle the problems of life through his experience in the home than from any other source.

The best introduction to life and living which any child can have is to be a member of a happy family. In the atmosphere of security and mutual service which prevails there he will learn the lessons which will not only enable him to live his own life worthily and well, but to cooperate with others. Good citizens are made in the home.

The time will come, of course, when the child will want to know how he came into the world. The wise parent will on no account deceive him. Many parents, who are anxious to answer a child's questions truthfully, stammer and blush and so convey to the child that he has stumbled upon something of an exceedingly awkward nature—something better not discussed at all, since even grown-up people grow all hot and bothered about it.

While it is of the utmost importance that the child should be told "the facts of life" as soon as he is interested enough to ask questions on this subject, it is far more important that he should learn, from his everyday experience of living in the family circle, that marriage and the family provide the keys to unlock all that is best in life.

Give to your children this precious boon and they will benefit from it as long as they live. And so will all those with whom they come into contact.

So far we have dealt with children in general, but something needs to be said regarding the effect of children on the lives of the parents.

The Waiting Period

It is natural and necessary for a woman to withdraw into herself during the latter part of the waiting period. Realizing she is pregnant, she knows that she is faced with the supreme task for which Nature has prepared her. Her attention, both biological and emotional, is therefore concentrated upon the creative process which is taking place within her. It is important that the husband should recognize that this is natural and necessary.

Hitherto she may have shared very fully in all the activities of the marriage. Now, she must curtail some of these activities for the sake of the child within her. This may be resented by her husband. If he complains—as some do—that his wife thinks of nothing but her forthcoming baby, he is merely displaying ignorance—and dangerous ignorance. For there is no time when a little extra attention and kindliness is more called for than this. No matter how much the husband may want the child, one thing is certain: the child cannot possibly mean so much to him at this stage as it does to his wife. True, some women tend to magnify their disabilities during pregnancy in order to gain added attention from their husbands, but very often what appears to be an attempt to secure attention for themselves is really an effort to insure ample attention to themselves *as mothers.*

On the other hand, if the husband's attitude is not markedly sympathetic and helpful, the woman may try to hide her feelings of dependence and seek to underestimate her temporary handicaps in order to avoid being selfish. She is particularly sensitive at this time and is usually exceedingly anxious to feel secure in her husband's love.

During this period the wise husband will take great care to be more than usually attentive and sympathetic, and not on any account to reveal irritation or resentment because his wife cannot be, first and foremost, a wife to him.

Particularly to be condemned is the attitude of the husband who, during his wife's pregnancy, seeks temporary friendships elsewhere. At a time when his wife's emotions are profoundly stirred, such conduct may produce repercussions which are severe and lasting. For the wife, the birth of the child by no means completes the task of motherhood. It has only begun and must continue for years. This obvious fact has its dangers to both husband and wife.

The woman, well aware of the supreme importance of her task, may tend to regard it as a life task, which of course it is not. It may be the biggest task of her life, but it does not last throughout life. She should, therefore, take care not to become *completely* absorbed in a task which is inevitably lengthy and exacting, but which should not cause her to forget that now she is both mother and wife.

The woman who completely identifies herself with her maternal duties, unmindful of the wifely tasks, not only renders her husband's life miserable and possibly unbearable, she also prepares difficulties for herself in the later years when her maternal duties are completed. She may feel that she is insuring for her children every possible advantage which she can give them, but in truth she is hampering their development by bringing them up with a faulty background. The interests of the children demand that the husband-wife relationship should be happy and strong.

On the other hand, men sometimes resent the inevitable large measure of preoccupation with the physical care of babies which falls to the mother. The most intimate contacts with the child fall to the mother. All this is right and necessary. But if a husband fails to recognize this, children may become a barrier, separating husband from wife instead of bringing them closer together.

The real test—the supreme test—of the success or - otherwise of a marriage lies in the happiness of the family. If parents and children are happy, the marriage can be counted successful, and the probability is that the children will also prove successful in marriage. In the happy home they learn all that matters, for they become accustomed by day-by-day experience to a working example of a happy family relationship.

DIFFICULTIES ON THE WAY

No two people can live long in the close intimacy of marriage without finding—even without looking—many grounds for complaint against each other. And if they have formed the habit of constantly being on the watch for such things they will find ample cause for constant lamentation!

It takes time for persons of opposite sex to achieve adjustment to each other. No two people are alike beyond the fact that both have failings. But two imperfect people may attain a perfect marriage relationship through complete adjustment to each other.

A man may be regarded as the type likely to make an ideal husband. He may be experienced and successful in most of the practical affairs of life. But whether or not his marriage is a success will depend entirely upon the measure of adjustment which he is capable of attaining to one woman-*his wife.*

Difficulties On The Way

A girl may bring to marriage all the qualities which men admire. She may have good looks, pleasing personality, and seem to the entire world the ideal wife for any man. But whether or not she enjoys the blessings of a happy marriage will depend entirely upon the degree of adjustment she attains to one man—*her husband.*

If all who marry could keep always before them the idea that their task is to achieve adjustment to their partners, at least ninety per cent of marital difficulties would be overcome. People tend to change in various respects. Therefore, in marriage we do not have to attain adjustment once and for all; instead, constant adaptation and re-adaptation is called for. It is a lifetime task in which gradual improvement is achieved if one really tries.

Facing Reality

Even those who are freer than most from romantic idealism generally nurse a few illusions which are suddenly broken during the early days of marriage. Usually, before marriage, the couples see each other at their best. Their engagement leads to a whirlwind of congratulations. Together they hold the center of the stage during their courtship, with everybody tendering compliments and offering good wishes.

Then, suddenly, all that is replaced by a totally different set of conditions. The young husband wakes to see what his wife really looks like first thing in the morning. Before then the wife has sampled the dubious joys of listening to her husband's unmusical snoring for the first time. Little things, of course, and inevitable. But they can produce irritation.

Hitherto the husband may have lived a carefree, happy-go-lucky kind of existence. Now he finds that his time is not his own to anything like the extent it once was. His wife, without the slightest intention of prying, naturally likes to know what he has done during the day. And whereas in the past she seemed to talk only of pleasant things, she now reveals that she has some very strong likes and dislikes.

The young wife who feels, naturally enough, interested in her husband's activities during the day may be inclined to assert, or over-assert, her claims. She may insist upon hearing details of all that has occurred, when he is tired and needs rest before being able to enjoy conversation. All sorts of little difficulties and divergences may arise. And neither of the partners can now run to others, particularly parents, for advice on every little problem. They have got to face reality. It forces itself upon them in a

Difficulties On The Way

hundred ways. And they have to face it together— as a team.

How you face up to reality, in the form of the everyday experiences of married life, is the real test of your maturity, which reveals itself in your capacity for understanding and your degree of adaptation. Learn how to handle this wisely and well and you have solved the problem of living together.

Mutual Adjustment

It is a good plan for both partners to try, during the early days of marriage, to understand as completely as possible the other's outlook and attitudes.

The reason why you study your partner's attitudes is that you realize that the biggest challenge of your life lies in him or her. Can you adapt your own life so that the things you say, do, and think help to bring you closer together? Can you learn, step by step, how to avoid unpleasant clashes of temperament?

It may seem very obvious that such questions as these should be repeatedly asked and answered by all who would make a success of marriage. But the truth is that most married people very rarely devote careful thought to such matters unless things are going badly wrong, and then it is often too late to mend matters.

This was recognized by one husband and wife who had drifted apart. They both achieved success in the outside world, the husband as a man of business and the wife as an actress. And years after they had been divorced the husband wrote to his former wife: "I often think, as I look back at the past, that if only I had devoted to my marriage one fiftieth of the effort I put into my work, things might have been different." And the lady replied: "I often think much the same regarding myself. What fools we both were!"

People are ready enough to take such happiness as comes to them. But few realize that the conditions which tend to produce happiness can be consciously worked for, and very often attained. And while most people are prepared to agree that their marriage relationship is the most important thing in their lives, few act upon this view. That, more than any other factor, accounts for the innumerable marriage failures.

Look at it this way. No one can foresee the difficulties which lie ahead in marriage. But we know for certain that they will confront us. The people who make a success of marriage are those who use difficulties to better their relationship. They turn them to good account because they always carry in their minds the thought that the success of their marriage is more important to them than anything else.

A wife may wish to pursue a certain course o£ action but may hesitate to do so because she realizes that it will put her husband to some inconvenience. She may think the matter over for weeks. Then, very hesitantly, she mentions the matter to her husband. Much may depend upon his attitude to her suggestion.

We will leave out of consideration the blunt refusal even to treat the wife's proposal seriously, which amounts to a fiat denial that her point of view is worthy of attention. That attitude is obviously incompatible with the idea of marriage as an equal partnership. But almost equally dangerous is an attitude of indifference on the husband's part. *"Do what you like; I don't care in the least!"* That kind of reply, especially in a matter which the wife regards as important, is very hurtful.

It is in little things like this that marriages often begin to "go wrong." Usually, the partners have no idea when or where the trouble really began. All they know is that they do not get along well together and that every day they seem to drift further apart.

A man may return home in the evening eager to tell his wife of the events of a day which has gone well with him. He may have been looking forward to seeing his wife's face light up as he related to her his account of some success which might mean an improvement in the family's position. If his wife—possibly with her mind full of domestic cares—fails to evince the slightest interest, let alone enthusiasm, he may from that day on tend to keep his work and his marriage in separate compartments of his life and thought.

In both these examples there may be ample excuse for the faulty tactics employed. There usually is, in fact!

The apparently indifferent husband may have had much to worry him at the time. He may have felt that he was acting perfectly reasonably in leaving the matter entirely to his wife, and was, indeed, actually paying a tribute to good sense in doing so.

As for the wife, the duties of home and family might have claimed sole attention if not outwardly, at any rate in her thoughts—just when she was expected to be interested in her husband's work outside the home.

But the point which matters most is this: in each case an opportunity to get closer together was lost. A

Difficulties On The Way

drift apart began—one which could easily have been avoided.

It will be noticed that although we have been dealing in this chapter with difficulties in marriage, not one word has so far been said about sex. Yet, in truth, all that has been said affects sex very closely. When both partners are all the time seeking to express their love by making a deliberate, conscious effort to understand, appreciate and encourage each other, the effect upon their sex relationship is inevitably profound.

The Right Background

The great essential is to provide a background of loving thoughts, deeds, and actions.

Of course, this appears very obvious when expressed in this way. But it is easy to overlook the importance of the right background when things go wrong. Because such feelings as irritation, disappointment, a sense of injustice, to name but a few, can exercise a prejudicial influence upon the sex relationship, and in fact usually do, it is often in this sphere that the results of a general failure to get along well together are most obvious. Even so, *the sex relationship is generally a reflection of the general relationship,* and not, as is often supposed, the other way round.

This is revealed by the manner in which, when "sexual disharmony" occurs, attention to faulty background factors often yields considerable improvement. Indeed, in a great many cases, once the general relationship is improved, so that friction and misunderstanding are replaced by companionship and loving understanding, the sexual difficulties diminish if they do not disappear.

A married couple feels that they have "changed." By this they mean that their physical union, which at one time was satisfactory, has become difficult or impossible. But actually they have not changed at all—not in any essential respect. They have simply acted unwisely and brought upon themselves the inevitable consequences of their course of action. Let us look into their case.

During the first few years of their marriage both partners saw much of each other and spent many happy hours in close companionship. Then the man seized a business opportunity, which resulted in his becoming increasingly engrossed in his work and having to spend much time away from home. When he was at home, his business claimed much of his attention. His wife found herself taking second place

Difficulties On The Way

to her husband's business in his thoughts. Left to herself more and more, she eventually decided to return to business, in which she had done well prior to marriage.

Eventually it dawned upon the husband that his married life was not all that could be desired. He determined to remedy matters. He was able to take things more easily than hitherto, and he decided to spend more time at home. But he found it impossible to recover the old sense of companionship. His wife, who had been an ideal companion during the early years of marriage, did her best to recapture the atmosphere which once had made the home so happy, but without avail.

These people's marriage had not failed, but they had virtually relinquished marriage in favor of something else—business. The same kind of thing is constantly occurring, although the interest which is placed before marriage may be different—sport, club, even work for some good cause.

People can drift apart when actuated by the best intentions. It is vital, therefore, to bear in mind that in marriage two people always have to be considered—not one. The man who feels called upon to embark on some form of social service which will necessitate his being away from his wife and home a great deal needs to consider very carefully whether or not there is a selfish motive behind his enthusiasm. Certainly he should weigh the matter with the probable effect upon his wife in view. The wife who throws herself into work for others, possibly welfare work, may become engrossed in it, and her home and marriage suffer accordingly.

It is of little use trying to adjust matters by being intensely loving for brief periods. The partner is apt to feel that he or she is little wanted in the ordinary way, and so cannot participate on the more intimate level. Always, the atmosphere created by the general activities of life influences everything.

What requires especially careful attention by those who would insure the right atmosphere in their married relationship?

1) *There must be no loss of individuality.* Neither partner must become a drudge or someone who is merely there; each must matter, and be encouraged to feel that he or she matters.

2) *The principle of equal sharing should be applied as widely as possible.* There should be sharing of work and leisure, of income and of duties, always in a spirit of mutual helpfulness and understanding.

Difficulties On The Way 119

3) *Great care should be taken to avoid any personal habits or mannerisms which irritate one's partner.* The fact that the habit may be harmless and trifling is beside the point; if it irritates husband or wife, it is important for that very reason.

4) *No important step should be taken without prior mutual discussion.* If this becomes habitual, it will maintain confidence and insure cooperation.

5) *Each partner should deliberately strive to promote the other's happiness in every way possible.* You have not only to do the right thing, but what is right for your own husband or wife.

Those five simple rules provide the means not only of overcoming the many inevitable difficulties which arise in even the happiest of marriages, but of turning the trials to good account. For it is by facing difficulties together, and in the right way, that love is strengthened.

One is tempted to leave the matter there, for the five rules given are certainly comprehensive and important. But suppose a husband and wife keep those rules well in mind and strive to apply them, and, indeed, constantly modify their attitudes or make allowances so as to insure reasonable harmony, is it not possible that both will feel a good deal of strain? May they not be aware that they are "making the best of a bad job" and that all the time things are by no means ideal?

Perhaps we should add one more rule:

Remember always to regard your partner in marriage as a total personality. Look upon him or her as a whole and take great care to include the good points as well as the bad.

This really takes us to the very heart of the matter. If only married people could be persuaded to carry this out, it would make a world of difference. There would immediately be a great increase of tolerance, a deepening of sympathy, a more penetrating understanding.

While it is of the utmost importance to avoid those things which are irritating to one's partner, it is even more helpful to attain a sound understanding of why such trifles—as they usually are—often produce so much annoyance and possibly even distress. Very few people are able to distinguish between surface irritations, of which we are all fully aware, and the deeper ones which are really much more important, yet of which we are usually unaware.

Difficulties On The Way   121

A husband may eat noisily, or may have a habit of whistling in the bedroom while undressing. Such habits are annoying in themselves. *But some men who do these things are loathed, and others loved.*

Some are loved in spite of their irritating habits. But are the others loathed because of their mannerisms or minor departures from normal good conduct? It is unlikely that *any* wife would wish her husband to whistle when undressing, or eat noisily. Why, then, is Mr. A loathed for his whistling and noisy eating, while Mr. B, who does these things equally well and equally often, is adored by his wife?

The answer is that in both cases the surface irritations are present, but that the response of the wives differs according to the nature of the deeper emotional attachment. If this is unsatisfactory, the feelings of discontent and disappointment tend to be concentrated upon the obvious faults and failings of the partner. On the other hand, if the deeper emotional union is happy, then even the most glaring faults, let alone minor irritating mannerisms, are often treated lightly, if indeed they are not regarded as near-virtues.

Very few people are entirely satisfied with the house they live in. Almost invariably there is something which is by no means ideal and which they would like to change. But we all take our homes as a whole. We are fully aware that there are certain deficiencies and inadequacies, but we should not for one moment think of condemning the whole structure because some of the details are unsatisfactory. If, on the whole, it serves its purpose reasonably well, we are satisfied.

But while most people are reasonably content if the house they live in represents ninety-five per cent of their ideal house, some married people seem to think that there is something hopelessly wrong with a marriage which does not represent at least ninety-five per cent of their idea of the ideal marriage. They expect their partners to be perfect, or so near to perfection as make no difference. If they can discover five per cent of faults and failings, this causes them to completely overlook the remaining ninety-five per cent of virtues.

If difficulties are to be successfully surmounted, it is absolutely imperative that a more realistic attitude than this should be adopted. And one way to acquire the sound attitude is to remember that the things which cause us to feel intensely annoyed with our partners are very rarely the real causes of our discontent. There is only one way in which we can find out what really is wrong. That is to stop

Difficulties On The Way 123

looking at our partners' faults and take a good look at ourselves—or, rather, *into* ourselves. The surface irritations which arise outside of ourselves are merely the symptoms—not the disease. That is to be found within our own make-up or in our basic relationship with the partner in marriage.

In actual practice, of course, most of the difficulties which arise are not clear cut. They often seem to appear suddenly, and for no particular reason, and often both husband and wife have not the vaguest ideas as to the cause.

Thus we often find couples "drifting apart." They are aware that things are not going well. They are conscious of a sense of disappointment. But beyond that they know nothing of the reasons for their troubles. Sometimes both husband and wife devote much earnest thought to the problem, but cannot discover what is wrong.

Act! Do not let things slide.

One piece of advice can be confidently given. *Act! Do not let things slide.* If you do, they will only slide one way—downhill, never up. They will go from bad to worse, and then to very much worse.

There is one form of action which is usually possible—a heart-to-heart discussion about the whole problem. Often this helps enormously. What one partner has overlooked, the other has often noted. Two heads are usually better than one in marital difficulties.

A couple who, as they expressed it, "always got on each other's nerves," was found on investigation to be suffering from extreme boredom. They were quite unable to mention any specific habit or attitude which annoyed them. They were both intensely anxious to please each other. And, indeed, they had probably carried this just a little too far in some respects, for they had become accustomed to a routine of smooth, cautious, polite, utterly inoffensive relations. There was no light and shade in their lives. They lived a dull, monotonous, somewhat dreary existence, with never a word out of place and everything so very correct that the atmosphere of their home rather resembled that of many a quiet boardinghouse.

This couple was certainly loyal to each other. Neither had any complaints to make regarding the other. Indeed, their extreme anxiety to do the right thing and to give no cause for offense provided the key to their problem. The consultant whose advice they sought was impressed by their obvious over-

Difficulties On The Way 125

anxiety in this direction. He realized that they were carrying a perfectly laudable attitude to extremes.

They were, in fact, always acting in a negative manner. Instead of seeking to give the utmost pleasure and satisfaction to each other, they were always much more concerned with giving no cause for offense. The mere avoidance of friction is not enough; there must be a conscious effort to promote each other's happiness and welfare.

The consultant surprised them. He advised them to give a little more rein to their true feelings.

"Don't be afraid to express, freely and frankly, your reactions to each other's conduct," he said. "You are both holding yourselves in too much. It might be good for you both to speak out more and each let the other know what you really feel."

This advice, tendered with some trepidation as a last resort, proved invaluable. That very same evening they had one of their most interesting talks for many a long year. The husband's eyes were opened to little selfish acts of which he was completely unaware—habits into which he had drifted and which, performed in the politest manner, had never seemed selfish before. The wife was astonished to hear how some of the things which she had done in the utterly erroneous belief that they would please her husband had really irritated him profoundly. This was all very helpful. But even more helpful was the way in which husband and wife, who for years had been boring each other, suddenly became *interesting*. They were no longer bored people. They were two lively, alert human beings talking about the things which really mattered to them. By opening their hearts to each other they banished boredom and ceased to be boring.

These people had not been neglectful of their duties or responsibilities. They had merely relied upon a faulty technique for dealing with the problems associated with their shared relationship. They may not have been aware that they had such a technique; indeed, they had probably never devoted serious thought to the subject. Some married people have a technique, of which they are fully aware, for dealing with their difficulties, and which they have consciously developed to enable them to manage their part of the marital relationship satisfactorily. These are probably the minority. They are certainly the minority where husbands are concerned, for usually they devote much less thought to such matters than do their wives.

But although only a minority of people have a method of this kind of which they are aware, all husbands and wives have some sort of system or

Difficulties On The Way   127

technique which they use for dealing with marriage difficulties. They may be totally unaware of its existence. But it is there just the same. They utilize it whenever difficulties arise.

This results in a-tendency to deal with various situations in a particular way. It may not always be applied, but every husband and wife tends, in general, to some specific rather than haphazard manner in dealing with the innumerable problems of the joint relationship. This fundamental system or technique is important. You should recognize its existence. *You should bring it under review from time to time, and especially when difficulties are encountered.*

You can largely prepare yourself to deal with difficulties by improving your system or method. You have to consider your own emotional make-up and that of your partner. You have to keep in mind the aim of mutual adjustment. No thought of domination, or of working out some method whereby you can gain advantages over your partner, must be permitted to enter. The whole object must be the strengthening of the relationship, thus giving love chance to thrive and grow.

Even if only one of the partners meets marital difficulties in this thoroughgoing manner, a considerable improvement often results. But if both face the facts fearlessly and frankly, and face them together, the results are almost invariably satisfactory. Honest self-criticism and frank discussion have saved many a marriage and made many a marriage.

Finally, let me reiterate, since it is of the utmost importance, that your partner must be considered as a total personality.

It is inevitable that two people, within the close proximity and intimacy which marriage entails, should at times jar and jolt each other. Well, accept that. But recognize also that both your own and your partner's real worth in marriage cannot be assessed solely by reference to the debit items—the faults and failings. Give full credit for the virtues, the loyalty, the day-by-day companionship, the regular services, small and large.

Most people—even those who grumble loudest— usually see things very differently when they look at themselves and their partners in this light.

DANGEROUS CROSSROADS

*I*s it likely that you may fall in love with someone other than your partner in marriage? The question is often asked. The answer is that much depends upon the sort of person you are.

Some emotionally unstable types are always falling in and out of love. They inquire pathetically—for they are always looking for sympathy—why it is that love constantly beckons them, only to leave them after a short time? These people of numerous "affairs" are incapable of genuine love. They are infantile in their outlook and always wish to hold the center of the stage. It may not be their fault that they are what they are. Life possibly has made them thus. They have been unable to grow up emotionally. We can sympathize with them but must not be guided by them.

Dangerous Crossroads

Sometimes these emotional babies marry, and when they do they are facing an impossible task from the start. They are embarking upon the supreme test of maturity, the life task which above all demands adult qualities, and they bring to it the emotional endowment of young children. While in this state they ought never to marry.

But some who do marry, and who are in many respects well suited to the marriage career, carry with them traits of an infantile character. In fact, we all do to some extent. And we have to guard against allowing these childish tendencies within us to get the upper hand. For if they do, they can wreck our marriage.

Temptations

Human beings are frail. It is as well to consider, therefore, what one's attitude should be if at some time or other temptation to break the marriage vows should be encountered.

First, those who have honestly tried to be the willing servants of love, and who have deliberately set out to attain adjustment to their partners in marriage, possess a valuable power of resistance. They have accustomed themselves to striving all the time to do the right thing. And thus they are less likely than others to succumb to temptation—or even to feel some of the temptations which may cause others to fail. They know the effort they have put into their marriage—the struggle to triumph over the many obstacles and difficulties which have been encountered. Consequently they are not disposed lightly to throw away what has been won.

Nevertheless, sometimes those who have tried very hard to insure the success of their marriage find themselves face to face with an opportunity to experiment, to venture in fresh fields which are off the route of the marriage journey. A man who has suddenly begun to realize that he is not quite as young as he once was is flattered by the attentions of a young woman. Or a woman who has feared that some of her former charm has left her may find a man friend unusually attentive and attractive.

It is a curious thing, but most of the books which contain guidance regarding the sex side of marriage have little or nothing to say about situations such as these. Yet nothing is of more vital importance than a sound technique for handling temptations. The right time for tackling them is—*right at the outset.* As soon as they are recognized, that is the moment to deal with them with resolution. Otherwise they may

Dangerous Crossroads

get a firm grip and become much more difficult to resist.

Marital infidelity seldom occurs suddenly, as the result of a temptation which comes quickly and is immediately accepted. Usually the married person sees the danger and debates with himself or herself whether or not to permit the situation to develop. It is hesitancy which causes the temptation to grow stronger, the attraction to increase.

The Erring Partner

This is all that can helpfully be said on the preventive aspect, but what advice can be tendered to those who are the victims of their partner's infidelity? Nobody who has read this article so far will expect one word of condonation for any offense against marital loyalty, and none will be uttered. But there are certain practical considerations which must not be overlooked. Circumstances vary considerably and it is impossible to be dogmatic as to what attitude should be adopted by the aggrieved party. If for a lengthy period it has been clear that one of the partners was finding the marriage tie intolerable, then a complete break might be the best solution. But in cases where the marriage has been on the whole happy, a single lapse should not be permitted to destroy all that has been built up.

It is often easier to tender this advice than to apply it. Both men and women suffer intensely from a feeling of injustice when, they themselves having been faithful, their partners deceive them. This is understandable, but the consequences of the breakup of the marriage must be considered. If the erring partner is prepared, even eager, to return, it is usually better to swallow one's pride, and this is particularly true if there are any children.

Here again love may have the final word. By its very nature love is forgiving. We all tend to find excuses for the bad conduct of those we love. If a love is so strong that even the infidelity of the partner cannot destroy it, love's sister—forgiveness—may enter. Forgiveness seems incredibly difficult at times. Yet "all have sinned and come short of the glory of God." And as we may entertain the hope that our own transgressions may be forgiven, may we not extend to our fellow travelers that merciful blotting out of iniquity which we would desire for ourselves? "To err is human, to forgive divine." Often that divine quality of forgiveness saves a marriage that would otherwise be broken up.

> Where forgiveness is prompted by love—and true forgiveness invariably springs from love—a marriage may not only be saved, but transformed into a much happier union than ever it was before.

Nor is that all. Where forgiveness is prompted by love—and true forgiveness invariably springs from love—a marriage may not only be saved, but transformed into a much happier union than ever it was before.

Here again the injured partner may well ponder upon all that has been said about the various emotional types, for therein can usually be found the explanation of the conduct which has brought a marriage near to breakup. Men particularly are weak and foolish in these matters. There is nothing to be gained by concealing that fact. Most women are well aware of it. But those who are emotionally strong, in the sense of being more mature, may well show mercy to those who are weaker. The undoubted fact that women are, in the main, more mature than men, would seem to account for the fact that women are usually much more ready to forgive a matrimonial lapse in their partners than are men.

Here, however, we are referring to women in general, and it may be asked how it is that sometimes women throw over all restraints and act in as irresponsible a manner as many men.

Women vary in integrity and in strength of character just as men do. Some of them are quite capable of assuming the liberty which men so often demand for themselves in sexual relations. Erroneous ideas, or the effect of some modern propaganda, may encourage them to adopt a frivolous attitude and to regard love and sexuality lightly. Where a woman acts in this manner she invariably experiences inner conflict, for she is striving to reconcile opposing loyalties. Her own deepest nature provides her with a code which is as strict and imperative as any set down on paper or in systems of morality, and is fundamentally important to her.

It follows that, unless a woman has little integrity she finds it exceedingly difficult to treat lightly the responsibilities of marriage. If she does, then she usually turns her back on her maternal role with all its implications, and smothers a deep, driving feeling of guilt with a defiant attitude. She becomes a rebel, driven on by a feeling of guilt and inferiority which surpasses that of most men, because it is fed by the knowledge that she has thrown away her birthright.

Divorce

Finally, a word about divorce. Those who fail to make a success of one marriage, which is but another way of saying that they failed to achieve adjustment to one partner in marriage, seldom make a success of any further matrimonial venture. Whether or not they marry again, they are often sorry that their first marriage was broken up. This has been observed by divorce lawyers, social workers, doctors, psychologists, and others.

Whenever a marriage fails, two people fail; and when they try again, they are attempting to succeed in something in which they have already failed. It by no means follows from this that those whose marriages have ended in the divorce court are necessarily doomed to fail in a second marriage, and indeed it is known that some whose marriages have broken down have remarried and been exceedingly happy.

Where the desire to break up a marriage is not mutual, the wronged party may remarry for companionship, but is usually reluctant to do so. Often it is the partner who wants the divorce who later remarries. There are very few divorces which are fully mutual. In most cases one partner wants a divorce, the other does not.

Divorce is always a tragedy, to be embarked upon as a last resort when all else has failed. It is particularly deplorable if there are children.

The only sound attitude toward divorce is to regard it as a necessary remedy in extreme cases, but as something which is *unthinkable* as regards your own marriage. Too many people have the idea of divorce in their minds right from the start. They see in it a convenient means of escape if things do not turn out well. Far better to concentrate fully upon insuring the success of your marriage, confident in your ability to insure this.

It is safe to say that if all who married did so with a firm determination to make their union successful, and sought from the outset to achieve mutual adaptation, the proportion of marriage

THE MIDDLE YEARS

The Halfway House of the marriage journey is usually reached when both partners are middle aged. There are, of course, exceptions—as when there are wide discrepancies in the ages of husband and wife. But generally speaking the "middle years" of marriage are also the middle years of life.

It is impossible to state precisely when this occurs. Some people are remarkably "young" at fifty, full of zest and enthusiasm and living lives crammed with worth-while activity. Others feel, and look, old at forty—or earlier.

But most people experience a slight shock while in the forties when it first dawns upon them that they are not quite as young as they once were! They find that younger people tend to treat them with rather more respect than formerly. They are conscious that physical effort is somewhat more tiring

The Middle Years 141

than it was. And possibly a glance in a mirror reveals something— perhaps no more than a slight thinning of the hair— which results in a long, hard stare into the mirror, followed by some perturbed reflection.

Some people take middle age in their stride. They accept it and they make the best of it, not deliberately and consciously, but easily and naturally. The reason is that they have learned to adapt themselves to life. They have learned to live. Consequently, fresh stages in life's unfolding, even this marking-time period after growth, can hold no terrors for them.

It must be admitted, however, that the majority, including those whose middle years are happy and in the best sense successful, are just a little disturbed by the first signs that middle age is beginning to replace vigorous manhood or womanhood. The man who has knocked up his century at cricket finds it hard indeed to accept not merely a tail-ender's place in the team, but the prospect of a seat in the pavilion instead of a place in the field. The woman who has raised a family finds it equally difficult to accept that henceforth she must retire from active participation and become a spectator. Not merely one or two things like this force themselves upon the attention; almost every sphere of life's many-sided activities is affected to some degree. No wonder that even the most balanced emotionally mature types find it all somewhat perplexing and a little disturbing.

Preparations for Middle Age

One of the unfortunate tendencies of today is that there is little or no encouragement to look ahead, at any rate after schooldays are past. The modern emphasis upon youth, and the many excellent organizations which exist to serve youth, tend rather to convey the impression that life ends at about thirty!

We have splendid facilities for vocational guidance of the young. We have a few agencies working to prepare young people for marriage. But we have no organization to assist people in preparing for their own inevitable middle and old age.

It is not suggested that men and women should devote a good deal of their time and thinking to the years that lie ahead. Unquestionably the best way to become the kind of person who will achieve happy adjustment to all that is involved in being middle aged is to live wisely and well reached. Even so, the sensible wife and mother will devote a little thought to the life she will lead when her family is "off her hands." The man who is very active while in the prime

The Middle Years

of life will do well to consider precisely for what kind of life he is heading when he *must* take things a little more easily.

It is failure to think on these things in advance which results in the feeling of intense frustration and uselessness which afflicts so many people in the middle years. They find themselves unable to do the things which they have become accustomed to, the things which they regard as, and which they have made, their very life.

> ...those who have really shared their lives will have made the best possible preparation for the middle years.

So far as marriage is concerned, those who have really shared their lives will have made the best possible preparation for the middle years. They will have learned how to eliminate, or at least reduce, sources of friction. They will have acquired the habit of talking things over together instead of merely arguing about them. They will have become accustomed to joint activities.

All these considerations are of immense importance in the middle years, for it is simply fresh applications of them which are needed in order to enhance the happiness and promote the welfare of both partners. When a man becomes a little less active than he was, when a woman finds her most absorbing interests (those associated with her children) withdrawn, the great essential is for the husband and wife to join forces even more closely than before and to discover new interests in life together.

But the things which are selected for such joint enthusiastic co-operation must be suitable. Nothing could be worse than to attempt, as middle-aged people, to "catch up on life," as it is sometimes expressed. By this is meant a deliberate attempt to recapture some of the delights of youth or early adulthood—to secure compensation for the years of home building and family raising. Nothing can be more pathetic than this. An occasional evening out together has much to commend it. A constant round of exciting pursuits, based on the attempt to act as though both are twenty years younger than they are, is a dangerous and undesirable form of escapism.

It is no use running away from life. It must be accepted. It is unavoidable. The problem is how to use all the years of your life to the fullest advantage.

Compensations

The first essential is to acquire a sound, sensible outlook upon middle age in general and upon the middle years of marriage. It is helpful to reflect upon the advantages which are associated with this stage of life. First and foremost, if you have not attained a reasonable degree of emotional maturity by the time you reach the middle years you probably never will, but you have almost certainly learned a very great deal. Not only has much knowledge been acquired, but the emotions have learned some useful lessons. You are almost—but not quite!—certain to be a more tolerant person at forty than at twenty; and by fifty the improvement should be even more marked.

Mention was made earlier of the keen cricketer who found himself relegated to a pavilion seat. But many to whom this has happened have found their services as advisers in great demand. Often there is a seat on the committee for such a man. And there are seats on all kinds of committees for the knowledgeable middle aged.

One of the dangers to be avoided at this stage is any tendency to "manage" others. There must be no undue fussiness or interference with others and particularly with younger people. But the sensible middle-aged man or woman who avoids these manifestations of self-importance will find a great deal of interest in striving to help others, and particularly younger people. Such help must be tactful.

When the children leave home and marry, father and mother will find this aspect very much in their minds. Naturally they will wish to do all that they can to insure the well-being of the young people. But experience will have taught them the dangers of interfering, or of appearing to do so, in the affairs of younger people, even their own children.

Fortunate indeed are the men and women whose children turn to them for advice and counsel. Needless to say, whether they do so or not depends mainly upon the kind of cooperation which has existed between parents and children throughout the years. The man who is intensely lonely in middle life and whose children never come near him or seeks his advice is invariably the one who, possibly without even being aware of the fact, built up a barrier of inapproachability. The woman whose children never turn to her for guidance once they are married is usually paying the bitter price for being too little attentive (at its worst, indifferent) or too attentive (at its worst, interfering). We reap what we sow and we

The Middle Years

> We reap what we sow and we begin to realize it more than ever in middle life.

begin to realize it more than ever in middle life.

One exceedingly valuable acquisition of the years which yields much comfort and serenity in middle life is what may be termed ethical maturity. This is partly the reward of earlier efforts to achieve mutual adjustment; and it can be enjoyed only by those who have become sufficiently freed from narrow self-interest to be genuinely interested in the welfare of others. Ethical maturity is not something which concerns only the partners within marriage; it is an all-embracing quality which affects all life's relationships. But it is of special significance and value in the middle years, for it is the key which opens the door to a wide variety of absorbing interests.

To a very great extent we create this quality of ethical wholeness as the years pass. It comes to fruition in middle life—or, rather, it flowers most copiously then.

Norman E. Himes, a well-known American writer on marriage and its problems, refers to the importance of a "benevolent attitude in contributing to marital happiness." He says:

"People who are interested in others besides themselves, who have strongly developed "other-regarding" sentiments, who have sympathies for the underdog, who are interested in social improvement, who rarely put their own interest first at all costs, possess qualities of character useful for adjustment in marriage. The reason is that they will consider with an open mind another's point of view. They are capable of sympathy; they are capable of understanding their mate's point of view because it is a part of their habitual thinking to put themselves in the places of others."

Clearly this quality—or combination of qualities-is of enormous benefit to any marriage. But the "habitual thinking" mentioned comes to few, if any, quickly. It takes years to acquire. Those who are wise enough to cultivate it possess it in good measure only after years of effort, of self-discipline, of failing and trying again. But in middle age we enjoy the benefits of all our previous self-discipline, just as we suffer from any lack of it.

One of the graces by which ethical maturity reveals itself is respect for the personalities and ideas of others. Mark well that word *respect!* It is something more than mere tolerance. It is not "negative," in the sense that we "put up with" a great deal with which

The Middle Years 149

we disagree. It is positive, warm, and encouraging, and happy indeed are those who have this power to respect the views and opinions of others, for it brings forth friendships. It yields a reputation for fair-mindedness and understanding. And it gives to us the precious power to bring out the very best in those with whom we come in contact.

Not many young people ever seriously attempt to analyze the qualities possessed by those they describe as "thoroughly good sorts." But instinctively they turn for advice and guidance to the uncle, friend, or parent who possesses the attributes of ethical maturity, which may be briefly listed as broadminded-ness, penetrating understanding, a strong sense of justice and an equally strong sympathy, complete objectivity in giving advice, a genuine liking for people as people, irrespective of position, race, or creed, and kindness in dealing with the troubles of others which is equaled only by the courage with which one faces one's own.

Baseless Fears

Far too many people approach the middle years with foreboding. They tend to assume that because they cannot do all that they formerly did, or live their lives at the same intensity, all is lost. A certain amount of readjustment is necessary. Given that, there is no reason why the middle years should not prove among the happiest in life. But both men and women often suffer needlessly through baseless fears.

The wife has the more trying time in many respects, for she is faced with the loss of her reproductive power and the loss of her children. Both these factors may weigh very heavily upon her.

In women the reproductive life lasts for some thirty years. It usually begins at or around the age of fourteen and ends in the middle forties. The woman who is prepared for a period of readjustment, who realizes precisely what is happening and is not worried by belief in old wives' tales about the dreadful consequences of the "change of life," should experience little or no difficulty.

That is true as regards the physical aspect. But it is hardly surprising that so important a change, the cessation of power to reproduce, should sometimes have psychological repercussions. These sometimes result in behavior which is totally different from that normally followed by the same woman.

For instance, in some cases, even before the physical changes have become apparent, wives sometimes experience a sudden "flare up" of sexual feeling. It is as though they feared that, if they did not

The Middle Years

avail them selves of the remaining opportunities, they would soon find themselves completely denied all sexual expression, therefore, they strive to make the most of the brief time left to them.

Sometimes this results in exceedingly unfortunate behavior. Sometimes, too, the idea that she is growing old may become an obsession. "My life is finished. I am now entirely useless. There is no point or purpose in living any longer" represents the attitude of some women who fail to adjust themselves to the "change."

Here let me emphasize that I am referring to extreme cases. Most women do not act in the way indicated. But the wise husband will gather from what has been said how necessary it is to be more than usually sympathetic and understanding during the period of the "change," and also to realize that this is just a passing phase.

Far too many men are ignorant regarding the emotional significance of the change of life in women. Therefore, let the husband note the following words of a woman psychologist:

"Just as at puberty she left childhood behind and entered a new world, so now, when the reproductive life is left behind, she enters again a new world, but *one which, when she becomes accustomed to it, holds infinite possibilities in the way of work, friendship, and satisfaction.* No longer will she live in her children, if she has them; no longer will she be tossed about from one pinnacle of emotion to another; the storms of her life are largely over. Henceforth she will sail in calmer waters."

The husband, for his part, does not, to the same extent, undergo the profound change which takes place in his wife. His own reproductive powers diminish gradually and he may attain the age of sixty or seventy before his reproductive life ceases.

Many men pass through a period of panic when they realize that their virility is diminishing. They see old age approaching, and an old age which is full of terrors. This sometimes results in extreme depression, or it may lead to attempts to have a "final fling" before it is too late.

Thus we see that both men and women may suffer in middle life because they fail to maintain a normal outlook upon life. They hold a distorted view of middle age. They conjure up visions of old age which are frightening and false.

The Middle Years

Avoiding "The Tragedy of Middle Life"

What is sometimes called the psychological tragedy of middle life can be avoided by almost everybody. It can be provided against in advance.

Those who have reached the age of forty, or at the most forty-five, should devote special attention to the cultivation of worth-while, wholesome interests outside of their immediate work, whatever it may be.

Here we see how important it is that the wife, no matter how busy, should try to maintain links of friendship and service outside the home. The woman, who, in spite of the calls upon her time, has remained a member of a church, club, or some other organization, is able in middle life to devote more time to these interests. But where the links have been severed it is by no means easy to make a fresh beginning. She is apt to visit church, club, or discussion group only to feel that she is a stranger, unknown to the members and they unknown to her. All of which tends to reinforce her feeling that she is useless and unwanted.

As for the husband, he, too, needs interests outside of his immediate work, and it is helpful if he bears in mind, when considering fresh interests or recreations, the fact that he will grow older as the years pass and not remain as he is. For some reason or other human beings have always found it difficult to appreciate this simple truth and its obvious implications.

The great essential is to maintain a normal outlook upon life, then old age need not come for many years, and even when it does it may prove a period of serenity and happiness. And the best way in which to keep a sound, sensible outlook is to have ample interests, many of them shared by husband and wife.

Here it will be noted that it is not suggested that all interests should be shared. They should all fit into the general plan and should not be irritating to either partner. But they need not, and should not, all be of a joint nature. For in middle life it is very desirable that both husband and wife should have their own friendships. This is indeed a period in which men tend to seek the company of their own sex, while women often turn more than formerly to other women for discussion and friendship. The cultivation of such friendships should be encouraged provided always that the shared relationship within the home is well maintained.

In early middle life it is as well to consider the financial position afresh with an eye to possible retirement, complete or partial.

The Middle Years

Planning for possible retirement must include careful consideration of the family income in later years and sometimes it is desirable to take out an insurance policy, the proceeds of which can either be taken in cash or in the form of an annuity. There are many different kinds of annuities. The one that is best for any individual depends upon the particular circumstances.

CAN RELIGION HELP?

"Nowadays there seems no point and purpose in our living. We just go on from day to day, aimlessly and miserably, whereas we used to have so much to share and do."

The woman who said that was trying to explain how her married life had changed since the war. And later her husband said this:

"I don't think I've really changed and my wife is much the same as she used to be. Yet we don't seem to have anything in common. There seems little or nothing to work for—we just carry on, without the slightest enthusiasm, well aware all the time that something is wrong."

This vague feeling that all is not well troubles many married people. They know that things have changed and they wonder whether the unsettlement in the outside world is not reflected in their own lives.

Can Religion Help? 159

They feel that they are the victims of the times in which they live. And they are right. For in a great many case this loss of a sense of common purpose springs from the widespread indifference to religion.

Take the case of the two people already mentioned.

During their early years of married life they had a strong interest outside the home which influenced their own home life profoundly. They both availed themselves of the guidance and encouragement which religion gives. Having been accustomed to religious observance since childhood, they continued after marriage.

But war, which destroys so many good things, changed all this. The husband intensely disliked the compulsory church parades which he had to attend while in one of the services. He felt that religion was essentially a personal matter and one in which compulsion was entirely out of place. Except when compelled by service regulations to attend church, he abandoned his former habit of regular attendance.

Like thousands of others, he and his wife ceased to take any active part in religious observance after the war. Yet when they came to look into the factors which may have accounted for their dissatisfaction, they found themselves compelled to admit that something vital, helpful, and exceedingly valuable in their marriage had gone with their loss of interest in religion.

To many people this may seem absurd, yet the facts are plain. Numerous investigations have been made into the factors which contribute to marital happiness and unhappiness. Both in Great Britain and in the United States it has been found that religion is a powerful factor in promoting the stability and happiness of marriage.

The difficulty is that, although we know perfectly well that religion can help, we cannot prescribe religion to all and sundry as though it were a medicine. Some people, in despair because "life" has gone awry, turn to religion hoping it will benefit them, and with no higher motive than pure self-interest. They are invariably disappointed.

You cannot "take up" religion. It has to take you up if its beneficial effects are to be felt in your own life and in your home.

But it is helpful to understand precisely why religion can be so powerful an ally in the cause of marital happiness, if only as a corrective to the far too common view that religion is an outworn relic of

Can Religion Help? 161

ignorance which can have no place in the enlightened days in which we live.

The lack of a goal, which accounts for the feeling of purposeless existence which is frequently experienced by those who fail in marriage, can be fully met only by a philosophy of life which makes our every thought and action significant, and which enables the weakest of mortals to link his own puny power with that infinite power which lies behind the universe.

The feeling of inadequacy, of utter inability to achieve anything worthy, can be banished only by putting in its place confidence of ability to achieve something worth while.

What but religion can provide these two essentials to the good life—a goal to be attained and confidence that it can be reached?

There is a constant ebb and flow in human affairs and this applies to religion as to everything that occupies man's heart and mind. And whenever religion is ignored, whenever there is widespread indifference, moral laxity is marked. And moral laxity is always the enemy of marriage.

But the opposite also applies. Whenever the claims of religion are taken seriously, men and women tend to order their lives with regard to the good of others as well as themselves. That is the essential difference which religion makes. And its beneficial influence is inevitably strong in the marriage relationship where the opportunities for co-operation and mutual service are greatest.

If you take away religion, what have you left? Nothing but dependence upon self and nothing but interest in self. The spiritual loneliness which is the plague of modern civilization is the inevitable consequence of forgetting that there are others in this world who matter besides ourselves. It is the natural result of denial, in men's hearts and minds and consequently in their actions, of the idea of the Brotherhood of Men. But how can we grasp this idea of universal brotherhood apart from the idea of fatherhood?

And once we accept the idea of the common Fatherhood of God, how can we fail to accept the view that all men, irrespective of their race or color, are our brothers?

No great movement designed to make the world a better and happier place in which to live but stands to gain impetus from such a lofty ideal as the common Fatherhood and universal Brotherhood. It is the one conception which, firmly held and logically

Can Religion Help? 163

applied, can assuage the ills from which humanity suffers. Can we afford to neglect it as a basis for marriage?

It is, indeed, within marriage that we may best apply the loftiest precepts and observe their results. You have not the power to remake the world on kindlier and nobler lines. But you may make of your marriage an ideal relationship between two human beings, and of your family an ideal community in miniature.

Happiness always lies in achievement—in worthwhile achievement. Ideal happiness never comes to those who deliberately seek it. Rather is it a byproduct of successful living. And no man or woman lives successfully who lives only for self. Show me an embittered, frustrated person and I will point him out immediately as one who is deficient in human relations. The power to live happily with others is lacking. The inner harmony which alone can enable a man or woman to meet the buffetings and trials of life without becoming soured is missing.

Nothing can restore it save acceptance of the essential truth that we are members one of another. This provides a sense of values, giving to us standards by which we can judge our actions and be guided in all that we do. It also gives us an understanding of the meaning of life.

Depend upon it; the child cannot fail to notice the lack of religious observance, or at any rate of religious inspiration, in the home. It is in the home that the child learns its most important lessons so far as the art of living is concerned. And if religion is to exercise its beneficial influence to the full in the life of the child, it must play some part in the home life. It must not be merely a school subject. It must be the motive power which inspires a happy family in a mutual effort to create a home in which each individual can develop character, and in which the growth of each furthers the happiness and welfare of all.

That is religion in action. That is religion applied in the home. A mere theoretical interest or habitual church attendance is not enough. Religion must be welcomed into the home and encouraged to thrive there so that love, the great redeeming and transforming force, can grow and bless all that dwell therein.

> Religion must be welcomed into the home and encouraged to thrive there so that love, the great redeeming and transforming force, can grow and bless all that dwell therein.

JOURNEY'S END

In the late years of life husband and wife find themselves drawn close together as they watch their children living their lives. The parents, as they grow old, live their lives over again in the lives of their offspring and find new joys and many thrilling adventures as they do so.

Younger people can hardly realize how large a part their every move plays in the lives of their parents. The weekly letter from son or daughter is eagerly awaited. Its contents is eagerly devoured and thought over. If one week it does not arrive, two old people may be plunged into gloom and anxiety.

What the psychologist calls projection plays a very important part in the mental and emotional lives of elderly people. The father sees his son striving to make his way in the world and he recalls the obstacles which he himself had to overcome. Just as old soldiers love to fight old battles over again, so elderly men renew the struggle for life—through their children.

As for the mother, she, too, is a spectator, but she is less detached than the father. Because her part in the birth and upbringing of the children has been much more intimate and profound than the father's, she feels every move her children make as though she herself were making it.

There can be no doubt that the richest joys which life has to offer the elderly are those associated with the family they have raised. Those who have stubbornly refused to have children, or who have unfortunately been unable to have them, often experience a lonely old age.

Some people grow old much earlier than others. Generally speaking, middle age should flow into old age without there being any sudden awareness of any profound change.

This is the more likely to occur if the partners have busied themselves with worth-while pursuits, particularly during the middle years. There can be no doubt that the elderly people who have a round of interests which keeps them reasonably occupied are much happier than those who have little or nothing to do.

Elderly people's services are likely to be in much greater demand in the future than they have been in the past, for a much larger proportion of the population will be over the most usual retirement age, sixty-five, than ever before. This will mean that full-time and part-time employment in a wide variety of callings is likely to be available to those who wish to continue working.

Economic necessity may result in greater encouragement being given to elderly people to continue to work.

Certainly there is everything to be said in favor of older people engaging in suitable work, possibly on a part-time basis, rather than spending their time in complete idleness. The sudden change to idleness, or something very near it, after a life spent in hard work, often results in profound depression. Many a retired pensioner watches with envy an elderly friend who still has to catch a train each morning in order to go to work.

But while it is desirable that the later years of life should include the interest and activity of useful work, this period is inevitably one in which contemplation plays a considerable part. Those who have lived a full life tend to sum up what they have learned. They think hard and often upon the

Journey's End

meaning of life. And the happiest old people have a philosophy. They may not be able to expound it clearly in words, but they possess it all the same, and it becomes of immense significance to them.

This philosophy of life, firmly founded upon lengthy firsthand experience, can provide much comfort and inspiration. It is the reward and fulfillment of that ethical maturity which we noted as being one of the most valuable assets in the middle years. And as with all life's greatest joys, its value is enhanced by being shared. Happy indeed are the old couple who together can look back upon a long life devoted to the upbringing of a family, who have sought together to teach the true way of life to the younger generation. Only one thing matters in those later years of life: *Did we do our best?*

> Only one thing matters in those later years of life: Did we do our best?

Those who look back over the years and see that, in spite of their many mistakes, their influence was invariably uplifting and ennobling does not worry about death. That is something which comes to everybody and it will come to them. Much, very much, has had to be faced in the past. And sufficient unto the need has been the power. Experience has taught them that they can meet every demand life makes—including its ending. They have learned where to look for hidden sources of strength. They are therefore unafraid.

Those who fail to achieve this firm grip on life's essentials are indeed to be pitied. They have merely done something which is dreadfully easy—based their thinking and living upon self-interest to the exclusion of all else. Thus in lives later years they have nothing to fall back upon but themselves—and they know that they are too frail spiritually to support themselves.

To be able to look back in life's eventide upon a life devoted to loving service and with offspring in their turn building homes in which love can dwell insures peace at the last. Having learned the secret of serene living, men and women can look death in the face and smile. They find at the end that this is all that matters. Only those who have learned to live are prepared to die. And the best school for living is marriage.

NOTES

NOTES

CPSIA information can be obtained at www.ICGtesting.com
Printed in the USA
237164LV00002B/180/P